A

~

Markus Sabo Gabriel

~

Freedom or Death

~

Ω

Bibliografische Information der Deutschen Nationalbibliothek:
Die Deutsche Nationalbibliothek verzeichnet diese Publikation in der
Deutschen Nationalbibliografie; detaillierte bibliografische Daten sind
im Internet über www.dnb.de abrufbar.

Verlag:
BoD • Books on Demand GmbH, In de Tarpen 42, 22848 Norderstedt
Druck:
Libri Plureos GmbH, Friedensallee 273, 22763 Hamburg

ISBN: 978-3-7583-3425-2

Markus Sabo Gabriel – Freedom or Death
The Destruction of the Patriot Movement

I The Destruction of the Patriot Movement

At the Edge of Time

Through all the ages, the enslavement of mankind, the truth was carried, like a subtle wind slipping through the holes of tyranny. This wind of revelation survived and after millennia metamorphoses into a heavy storm blasting the call for freedom.

Human history has been so far an endless tragedy full of myth, smoke and mirrors. And every generation failed to comprehend the mistakes of its past generation and continued, following the same patterns, that led to misery and wrongfulness.

By means of destruction and consolidation the hidden hand that formed all this chaos and confusion, managed to manipulate us closer and closer towards an interlocked worldwide machination that works clockwise. The nightmare of the old sages and folk sayings, even the words of the witness of the end-times as written in the bible, is played out right in front of our eyes. The Deceiver of mankind comes with a smokescreen of proportions and in a fashion and perfect planning which is breath taking. Measures that could only be concocted in the wickedness of the worst of evil minds, or the one all absorbing minister of malediction. For this force of true evil is not here to make any concessions, it is all around us and all absorbing. And we all will have to face it, whether conscious of it or not. Whether we are awake or asleep. The time for making a decision has come, there are two choices freedom or death. Nothing in between is offered, for the legions of death are in the total and freedom is just a choice.

However there was this storm in the background of souls and the unknown of the subconscious collective mind of mankind, which prepared the legacy for all those that went before us and tried to go against this end. Time after time and age after age, there have been uprisings against this system of mortification. But the heroes were buried like falling trees that leave no sound nor trace. Indeed very few survived the telling of time and even those that survived all the covering, are just dim reminders of the dreams of the past, an endless story of victories that were fought for unrighteousness over the just and righteous.

For all of you that are without courage for the fact that we seem to be outnumbered and the enemy might be in a better position or planning, let it be said that their dealings can be calculated but our intuition and genius cannot possibly be foreseen.

At the edge of time. We are here now in the present. But are we aware of all what happened, its reasons, its ramifications? How did we get to this point? For if we were, we would act different and there would be another tune of world history right now.

Over centuries Britania was prepared to be the center for the New Age to come. So the Scottsman Hammer by the name of William Wallace, could only be a very inconvenient obstacle in the minds and hearts of the past rulers, they were determined to raise the sails of future generations. This far back goes this planned conquest of what our generation now is to be witness. A unification and isolation of Scotland in a patriotic way would have been shattering or at least would have produced vast difficulties, for the ambitions of the cabal.

In the times of Napoleon and with his punishment of exile, which was to be seen as an act of "mercy" by the elite that dominates this world until today, by the name of Britania; the decisive crossroad was passed for the western world. People that pretend to be generous and of a character of fair play, when behind the scenes this very elite has made the decisions that paved our ground. But like a banker its all just a suite they wear, to pretend to be something which they clearly are not. But the crossroad was crossed with the end of Bonaparte or even during his reign, the west undertook the path to abolish the old system of rulership by an upgraded system of concealed rulership. Where the crowns and titles were to be switched by the impressions of a new deal for freedom, by actors in ties and suits. This move and revolution, or planned evolution was finished with the fall of Adolf Hitler. After WW II a complete new world was to be formed, after the destruction of this bold undertaking.

And most of the kings were in the end just pawns in the hands of the masters of destruction, and chao et ordo. And every leader that came to the scene who knew that it was Britania who ruled for so long the destiny of the world, especially in France had to be replaced. For the Frenchmen have always been suspicious not without justification of that very British elite.

My inspiration for this work is, that it is needed right now and in the near future, to lay a foundation, for the right decisions and actions to be made, by all those that are in hope for a better future and salvation. And also are willing to work towards freedom and salvation.

So I will try to formulate the many ideas that come into my mind into something that is more than powerful.

It shall be a manifestation for what was written into the stars and has no words to be mentioned properly; much more than an uprising, rebellion or revolution. But a last stand against everything that went wrong forever.

Ignorance killed the truth, Ignorance murdered truth throughout the time, so much happened but the ignorance of the people still remains and kills everything, it is truly the root of all evil with respect to the knowledge of Plato.

How much attention is given to babies and we were given when we were kids? But as we grew up, we became less and less important. We have become a wheel in a corrupt structure. Just to serve and fulfill our own supposed destruction. We are doing it by consenting to be nothing and worthless, and ignorant. When just like when we were born, we are still unique and powerful, we are giving our power into a vacuum to be absorbed, into some miraculous power-vacuum, which absorbs society. But everyone counts and every single voice does so. Every thought and action can be put into a wide ocean for the benefit of all, without being forced to do so. And everything in the world is done to prevent you the individual, to be unique and worthy and self-confident, that would be the end of main-stream corruption.

We live in the "Victimized Society", but we have been living in such forever and ever. We are supposed to put our sacrifice onto the altar to be burnt by furious psychopaths, that long for nothing more than for the lust of torturing and suppressing the people.

And just in the same way an automation is used, people get used as automation, by the elite, which is full of such characters, who in a natural order of things would be subjected to being sorted out and rightfully being ignored by the people.

The self proclaimed friends of mankind organized into fraternal orders, can state that their goal is really:

"We believe in the fatherhood of God and the brotherhood of man!"

"We take good men and make them better men."

False statements made by members of the order of the Eastern Star, belongings of Astarte and her principles and not of their supposed fellow-humans, which they pledge to serve. It is all but a show for those that are subjected into such circles to be corrupted and for those outside that might be dazzled by just looking with interest, into such carefully from the outside into the inside hidden circles. Your getting the point.

For everything that needs to be done in the dark is to be condemned by the outsiders, so they better not know of it. It is all just "Royal Faggotry", all their proceedings and the costumes they put on.

After much talk about the so called "Illuminati" and their secrets, it has become a fashion, that stars are shown, who allegedly expose this construct of which is little known, but really just take it and distort it into all directions. Those that are part of that organ had to act because, more and more information about that secret formation comes into light. One good example is the comedian Jim Carrey. But its not a comic anymore if you misinform and mislead people in the way this character does. It is clearly made to disable the mind. He takes a serious topic and leads it into fake and pseudo-notions, for dummies these thoughts, appear to be intelligent, but for the awake it is ridiculous and absolutely disgusting. It does not lead to any information that the mind could absorb to learn from it. He makes a big joke of a serious question and darkens it with false notions. Remember the song "Light in me" by Burnell K. Herring Jr., the guy represents those in power and into the face of the uninformed listener he preaches the gospel of the sinners. Everything that was forbidden by our Lord and Savior. An instinct of enlightened predators, that are really drinking blood and are cannibalistic.

Because in the kingdom of the BEEqueen, you have to take a side either you are a bee or a drone, there is nothing in between, not all along the so called watchtower, not in our time not in any age. Bureaucracies and officers have replaced the old buffers of the knights in older times.
Just similar to India with its caste-system, we are living in the west in a society that is dominated by the caste. The only way to rise to an upper caste is to compromise to corruption

or adapt to chaos and conformity. Their is a big difference between being a part of the Astor aka Astarte dynasty or been born into a slum, or entering a country as immigrant.

Because those that live in mansions, and have people subjected underneath them, that do all the work and supply them with all they need, have a complete different worldview and look downwards towards the rest of humankind, who are to them really just "peoples", or clearly spoken nothing. There is an absolute class-system established in the west, and those above the average, are completely excluded from the rest of society. And this kind of people will never stand up for the masses, because that would endanger their own positions of privilege.

The muses very often portray it in this way: the world is dominated by evil forces and wicked spirits, that control people, who then are enslaving others and drain out their blood. But in the dark there is the existence, of secret and benevolent orders, that are working to protect the small man and woman. What they do is twisting reality into a mirror world of illusions and opposites.

This system of absolute delusion and corruption is only protected, because of the massive ignorance of the majority. It helped to build a shield, behind all evil can be hidden, remember the words of Eric Blair alias George Orwell, "Ignorance is Strength", that is the slogan for the crowd. And confronted with the truth, there is no possibility anymore for arguing about critical topics. The democratic Anathema of confronting controversy is dead and buried. But the vital ingredient for a democratic society. So the real truth is now buried by slogans and brands. The word

Illuminati is replaced by Deep State. Confronting the fact that the earth cannot be possibly measured as by the Freemason Copernicus, is termed with the stupid word Flatearth. Visualizing the horrible picture of the middle ages, and the topic is dead by the second. We cannot look into the holy bible and find the answer, written down by men guided by God himself. The very God who created the earth should have known how to give that knowledge to his people. The Illumination process of the 18th century ended in the enslavement of the Massmind of humanity into a Borg like. **Alan Watt** said roughly, <u>as if knowing the truth would make them guilty of something</u>. Without the ignorance of the people, this system could be attacked from every sight and be destroyed like paperwork.

And so we will face the ending of the quest of the Masons to rebuild the temple of Solomon. Face Jerusalem and the destruction surrounding this event will usher in the end of times.

~

I The Destruction of the Patriot Movement

~

Patriotic Destruction

The cabal was able to prevail over so long from generation to generation, for one reason is that every uprising was shattered at their hands.

The biggest uprising against the goal to establish a system of worldwide everlasting Communism, was without any doubt the Patriot Movement. America the only country in the world and a lot of Patriots still owning firearms. The nation with the most researchers, teachers, authors, talk radio hosts on this subject. It produced a lot of documentation regarding the goals of the cabal. And it all started already before the killing of John F. Kennedy, with groups established such as the John Birch Society.

It has become a lesson for some of us, but all that are willing to maintain their freedom in times of hardcore despotism and arbitrary rules, should also understand this.

The cabal has always been at least one step ahead of us, and everything which could disrupt their plans, was already calculated precisely into the future back when the first fissures appeared, after WW II with quiet extraordinary authors who were exposing the hypocrisy of the "Fabian-System". The death of Kennedy at their hands who stated at his inauguration, that his work would be the freedom of the people, not democracy. That execution did manifest, that there is a cabal at work at the highest echelons of power.

How was the Patriot Movement destroyed or fragmented? Their horses in this race were a complete and very sophisticated network of Counter Intelligence Actors, the paranoia built up around the Edward Snowden revelation, talk radio was purged and there came a Trump into their hands, a nice Trumpet to deceive the so called patriots. If they really were made of patriotic blood, they would have never fallen for this cheap character. After a few months it was clear that it all was just an act. He had the better campaign rhetoric written. Some of you might think this guy is a douche bag, then looking back into confusion that is your future.

Before we continue with this example of how the Patriot movement got temporary disabled, because it is not buried yet. I want to define the term patriot and its true meaning.

The word Patriot comes from the Greek word patera – the father and there is the word patrida – the homeland. A patriot stands for his ancestry, the land his fathers lived and died for, the family and his people that make up the "Patrida". It is a proud word and has always been a high morale value, because if you have no freedom on your own ground, you have nothing and you are going to be nothing, because everything will be taken from you. Your freedoms, your rights, your belongings and family. This is what every freedom loving archetype has lived and died for from Moses to Leonidas, and from Wallace to Kennedy.

The destruction of the Patriot movement could be most likely brought about, by the fact that it will be shattered into a fraction of Trumpers who follow the Pipe Piping and the real patriots.

All who follow Trump are nothing more than nationalists. We have to separate a nationalist from the patriot. A patriot is a person who reacts only to threats, he does not threaten others or endanger other people. A patriot is reactionary. But a nationalist is much more an "Actionary", he takes actions, he was previously agitated or deceived by a demagogue. The portrait of a patriot was demonstrated now lets portray the nationalist.

All nations have been build on the grounds that elite figures set borders on the chess board of politics, were previously folks were living on the land of their ancestors. The family became a tribe and the tribe was afterwards ruled by a king or chosen of the people. The watchmen and builders of societies took that and created nation-states, which is not something that came into being naturally. No, it was created, crafted artificially with coat of arms, flags, banners, national-hymns, football teams and so forth. The tribes became kingdoms, the kingdoms nations and the nations will become unified continents, and finally a world-state. The new world order taken step by step as proclaimed by the older Bush.

Patriotism is natural, nationalism is artificially made, and can be used by demagogues to be transformed into national-socialism – Nazism, everyone should know that. Thus Trump could be brought in to establish a National-Socialistic state on the grounds of the United States, which then would be destroyed just in the way Nazi-Germany was destroyed. And finally they would say look what your nationalistic sentiments brought you, lets abolish all nation-states in favor of a communist world state, and all will live in equality and prosper under slavery. That is one possible Scenario for the future.

For now we know that the cabal took another path they moved towards Biden, meaning Communism, the final goal. The charade around the change in the naval-office was done to agitate towards a civil war of the left against the right. It will be difficult to convince the left to move to the righteous. But we should at least try to reconcile those that were dazzled by the Trump with the real patriots. A nationalist stands on a ground of deception, but he has a ground underneath his feet which is an artificial nation (the revolution was betrayed by the Nation State – the Union Jack), the leftists have nothing on which they stand; because socialism as state system, was from the very day it originated in the mind of Plato just a tool for the powerful. It has never been about brotherly love, justice and equality. But to the ignorant its like mothers milk, they have succumbed to it.

The same applies to the different churches that have been established into a church network. The churches just like the nation-state surround the christian with a building that is throned by a watchtower of the watchers, there are crosses of deception, olibanum, and clothed priests, that preach mostly the gospel of sheepherders. Its a network of artificial institutions, and institutions that have influence are ruled by the dark one, the one that wanted to deceive the son of man in the desert, and he showed our lord that he was in control of every institution on earth. So why would it change after 2000 years? Did the endless wars and suffering end? What are their fruits? What have they accomplished? The churches and the priest. Do they teach the bible as it is supposed? Have they been representing Christ in a positive way? Did they prepare the christian properly for the end of time? All they did was repeating dogmas, and destroy the name of Christ and Christianity by their wrong doings. So that every atheist could say, look what that pope did, or look at the corruption of this bishop. That is their fruit and labor in general and nothing else.

Irish Heartbeat

No one is allowed to claim to be proud about his ancestry anymore to get back to the topic of patriotism. And if you talk too much about ethnic traits and such you are a sub-human and national-socialist. Your suddenly marked and branded animal like. But those traits are in the blood. Every tribe had their own characteristics. They were given to their successors. And every folk had to live under different circumstances so forming a type of mentality. And that is the character of every folk and every people. For man was only allowed by God to live eternal on this earth by transfer of his blood to his offspring. And that is what you got from your ancestors. You are the result of what is left of endless struggles for survival. It is in your blood and that is some of the blood who poured through the veins of your fathers thousands of years ago, when the first names of tribes appeared. And now your not allowed to talk about which is important and what makes you up. Its racism! Is it really about race? Always remember sociologists invent words, that twist reality and rob you of your very humanity. And that is what you are made of blood and flesh, and in the blood is your soul, the soul of your forefathers who live now through you on this earth. No one should ever be ashamed of his folk and sublime it to an ideology which was to absorb all mankind into an equilibrium like machinery, where there is no difference anymore between language or kinship. When we talk about differences of ethnic traits, it is not about being a racist, it is about acknowledging the differences and many colors that paint our world. But you the real fascist, for you its all about pointing out the finger, with your plastic moral high ground. Because you have to force everyone into the all absorbing notions of conformist-language, acting, thinking and behavior. That every allegiance to kinship is to be labeled as Nazism. It is again just a twisting of reality. Every culture has to be destroyed in favor of a global-fetish culture of artificial plastic-people, which one day will be happy to have become something like the Borg. But the Irish heartbeat is drumming and again it is the Irish who stand up first against the measures of despotism. That very folks who keep the traits of their ancestors that can not be deceived.

We have established the notion of the patriot who is natural, nature was made by God and the human in the image of God. Now lets turn again to the techniques that were used to demolish the resistance against totality.

Counter Intelligence

Counter Intelligence is used to spy, infiltrate and break everything which is a threat to the system, means those in power, the Plutocratic-Olympians. Many centuries ago the Jesuits and the Rosicrucian were established by the old Olympians for different reasons. The Rosicrucian were a semi-secret group and Protestant-Christian-Front for the Illuminati. They put out extraordinary writings and acted under pseudonym to conceal, who really wrote about topics such as alchemy, poetry or literature. Even Martin Luther the great "Reformer" must have been part of that group, if one considers his coat of arms. So their influence on society was huge it included religion and everything that formed culture after the middle ages, and the shift towards a new system. This new "open" system needed some tight control. So it was the role of the Rosicrucian to be the unknown Muses for a new age to be build. They prepared the culture and the mindset for the future. But out of the Catholic Camp came another more secretly and viciously operating society, it was the Jesuits founded by Ignatius de Loyola. They call themselves the society of Jesus to wrap that sheepskin over wolfclaw. Their purpose was to spy, infiltrate and shatter every venture taken, that could threaten those in power and the system itself, and of course prevent every unwanted progress or innovation. They were trained to go into any kind of group, be it Catholic, Protestant, Jewish or else. The Jesuit Agent would be trained to pretend to be part of that very group he was to spy on, infiltrate or take over. So they put on a mask to conceal their missions of destruction. So the Jesuit Order was training spies, and part of a specialized elite system of intelligence gathering, under the facade of being part of the clerical structure. Is there any better way to mask yourself? Everyone had to fear to be betrayed by a Jesuit spy and be punished by the authorities. In the 18th century the Jesuits became so unpopular and infamous among all strata of society, people were really disgusted by them. You can even read this in the letters of the members of the "Bavarian Illuminati" (The Illuminati Perfectibilists). Where man who were recruited by Weishaupt, were asking over and over again to be sure, that the new group formed by Weishaupt would not be under the influence of the Jesuits, they had become really sick of them. Adam Weishaupt formed the new secret-society because the Freemasons were not viable to be used for leftist revolutions. And the Jesuits had become too unpopular. Weishaupt himself came out of a Jesuit school. What does this imply? The Jesuits were already influencing different secret-societies all over Europe and in the colonies, and could always return with new names and structures, which would use the same techniques of infiltration and information gathering. The same way the "Bavarian Illuminati", was restructured after its revelation and condemnation, by the Bavarian authorities.

The Bavarian magistrate was writing notes under the letters of Weishaupt, accusing him to be a foul deceiver of Christians who were completely fooled and used by this character. So Weishaupt a Professor in Ingolstadt (his cloak) was acting as a kind of "Spykingpin" for the central commanders of the Vatican. The Jesuits were a shock-troop for the system, to keep top corruption going and power flowing.

In this way by using two societies, Jesuits and Rosicrucian, the power structure was able to maintain control over the people under a new system offering in general more freedom to the masses, a shift from the old feudal system to another system, still under the control of a caste system of nobility, clergy, rich merchants and bankers. It could be maintained quite easy because of the division of the church into two main camps, which would fight each other, divide et impera at working. The Rosicrucian a Protestant Front and the Jesuits a Catholic, building a double face serving the same Master. At the very top there is an alliance.

We know that Elizabeth the first had a spy network at her disposal. So there was a network of spy agencies at work to inform and alert the upper class of any suspicion. So follows the thesis that the "Gunplowder Plot" to be executed by catholic men in 1605 was just a false-flag style attack, they were eager to change the situation in their own country which was Protestant, and to do so planned to blow up the House of Lords in London and kill a great part of the English Elite. But the king was informed of the plot by a chain of "miraculous" circumstances. Guy Fawkes who was ready to blow up the enormous building, was arrested, tortured and the rest of the band under the leadership of Robert Catesby were hunted down. The men were apparently used as patsies, the plot was even marked as Jesuit-Plot, and hence this was probably a Jesuit double play, because at the very top they are all in one club. Fawkes and Catesby were deceived, used and killed to further an agenda of prosecution in England. It would further the split between the two denominations, for generations now the English celebrate this failed attempt to the very day.

This secret networks would also spread to the United States, people out of the highest ranks were in connection with the successors of the "Bavarian Illuminati" in Europe and established Skull & Bones, out of this secret order, came the CIA. Which is nothing more than a modern Jesuit-Style apparatus of huge influence and destructive potential. So there is a link, an arrow between the Jesuits, the "Bavarian Illuminati", Skull & Bones and the CIA. Try to remember this chain because it will be important in this chapter and what you are going to read.

I say "Bavarian Illuminati", because this was just one sect established for a special purpose. People think that this is the real Illuminati, no it was not, it was a secret-society who came out of it and not the whole structure of the so called "Illuminati". Its important to understand such things for many only scratch on the surface and fail to comprehend the grand implication of the whole workings of the cabal.

Spy networks are a tool for the elite, they work out counter-intelligence and use shock-troops for means of disruption. Counter-intelligence is a construct which combines all measures to disrupt and spy on us "the enemies of the state", the so called "terrorists", everyone who is not of the same fascist opinion poured out by the main press. It uses agents, trolls and different leaders for different groups to destroy any opposition to the surrounding insanity. They can be used for purposes of defamation, of information that is put out by people that care for the truth. They can be sent into demonstrations to start rioting and so justify police brutality. They collect information and infiltrate grass-root foundations. George Bush the younger said it blatantly, everyone who is against us is a terrorist, means against the inner circle and everyone who supports fascism. That is the attitude of the Plutocrat towards people that want to keep their freedom.

The author is going to focus now on the most important things to be understood about the counter-intelligence and its shock troops at work. And also how they did work against the Patriot Movement in the US and the general uprising worldwide.

Shock Troops

Bullshit Artists

Let us begin with the cointellpro fraction, the heroes and leaders of movements for every group, there is a supply of those "Bullshit Artists", the name Bill Cooper invented. About Bill Coopers killing there is not much known. They buried him. He was admired and he wrote a good book, and the author learned a few very important things from him. Still the proof is there, that he could have been a plant, he was lying to people, deceiving, talking in a way down to people, always speaking in a very authoritarian way.

He was claiming to have infiltrated the Freemasons. This is so ludicrous. How did he do that? Then he would invite a young guy his "soldier" and tell his listeners, that this guy was into a masonic lodge. As if it was that easy to get into it. They would not even let me film the entrance from outside, when I went to the Grand Lodge in London. In the United States the Freemasons declined in the last few decades, they are willing to recruit new people but until you reach the ranks where you get real information, you will be corrupted and entangled by them. Sometimes he would talk in a double-tongue language. The stuff he was putting out was mostly very sophisticated. Much more than Alex Jones of course. And on his show have been quiet a few great guys, they would give good information. For example one guy from Arizona, said back in the 90s, that Austin was always a hotspot for the so called yuppies, snobs and the intelligence agencies. He said Austin Texas was never the real Texas, that was not the patriot high ground, right from where Jones is acting. If you watch the early stuff of Cooper and how he spoke to people, it should be enough proof for accusations. In one presentation he made the devils sign with his hand, and it was not accidental, it was done deliberately. Right into peoples face, and we have seen Jones do the same here and there. His supposed background has also to be questioned. He said that as a boy he went to a masonic boy lodge and that could have been the reason for him to be a witness of some strange things he saw, during his time in the military because he was led into the ... research.

His wife of Asian origin, his kids do not look like him, because this is very often the case, with mixed couples. Well the author might be wrong here, but to me it seems all to be a make up. His story, his background, his family. He acts with the best techniques. So it really looks to me as if he was forced into the Patriot Movement. There is a great possibility that he turned his back on the Agentur from 97 onwards. He would have been a dangerous person to the system. If he was killed in the fashion it was reported, that would make the whole incident a quiet repugnant act. But how to find out the truth of what really happened to him and his family?

Bill Cooper is not the main issue here, and the main problem, there are others, but the author wanted to share with the reader, what he found out about that person, and he does think its important to look into it as part of the scheme. How these people are trained and what techniques they use. The way they depict them self to their followers, how they are in need to get the followers trust them.

My theory on this case is that Cooper was probably compromised in some way, so they used him for the purpose of informing and deceiving the patriots. Later when he started to cut the strings above him, first they attacked him, and later did kill him.

There are spies that collect intelligence, because it is based on information, which they have to collect from the anarchists of the very right to the hyper fascists of the far left, the Antifa.

And information about the "enemy" gives power over the subjects.

Every fraction gets served by heroes and leaders. Lets go through some of those Bully Artists.

The author had contact with quite a few, so there is experience. They are schooled how to behave. They can disguise their viciousness much better. Their gesture, facial expression and posture its all a training. Evil persons can not really hide their wickedness. They reveal themselves to experienced persons in the way they behave. But Cointellpros, they can, they can be very cool and neutral. If they notice that you are quiet above the average and make a difference, then they really get interested in you, or very careful what they do in front of you. Now lets depict some of those that are working for the spy-network. Some of them reach many people and some just a few thousand, so it works like a shotgun fired at a target. There are the big guys like Judas Jones and smaller ones, that spread out from the center to the outside, just in the way the ammunition of a shotgun hits. In this way you can deceive and fraction in a maximized way, as many people as possible. The smaller agents will accuse the bigger ones of being such and more paranoia and insecurity will spread. But at the same time they will agitate people and put fear in their hearts.

A real Bullshit Artist for the Anarchists, is <u>Stefan Molyneux</u>. There was a guy who was believing that the Earth is not a globe. Now he was debating Molyneux about this, and Molyneux is supposedly of the opinion that the earth is a globe. That young guy was a real fan of Molyneux and very much demoralized by the fact, that his Guru was of a different opinion. Molyneux was standing with something plugged into his ear, getting information from an invisible guy on the other side, to counter that young guy; who was naive but bombarding him with proof of the earth not being a globe. It was ridiculous and disgusting to watch Molyneux being in need of explanations, because the truth can not be buried. And there he was standing like a bad actor, trying to win the debate. Trying to convince this youngster, that he is wrong. When the youngster was convinced. In a situation like this where a cheap artist like this, is telling you lies, there you got him, if they defend lies, they are on the other side. Molyneux was very much trying, to denounce his own fan, to his listeners to be just a stupid juvenile. But really he was going through a rightful waking process.

There is plenty of them for the Christians. It is enough if they tarn as Christian and preach the King James bible of which they know so much, they formulate a few creeds enough to catch the lambs by the wool. They start interpreting every word and every sentence in a way which is for me as Aramaic speaking person not nice to watch. Because they know nothing of the language in which the bible was written. They are making a lot of mistakes easy to figure out by every Jew or Aramean, speaking that language. You can have hundreds of different pseudo-smart interpretations for one bible verse. Some of them are just into it to make huge money. And then they go off chatting about the Trump being a savior but the lies have short legs. Some of them are saying that it is all a conspiracy of the Vatican, they want to reach an audience of general Protestant people, and then you have Catholic accusing the Protestants. There is even some that will tell you that it is all the fault of Calvinist, or it is a sole Mormon conspiracy hatched out altogether in the state of Utah. Fritz Springmeier however is a teacher in bible lessons and a man not to be deceived. For the so called "Flat-Earthers", there is this English guy, he calls himself Allegedly Dave, the name alone stands out. So he is allegedly Dave? His story is this: he had a good job, a nice sports car and a convenient house. He was an overweight upper-middle class guy, who then woke up to the threat, and now he is there to help people, and a symbol for an option to build a society parallel to the one we live in. Of course there is a picture of him with a dog like true true face, this guy would never lie to you. Again you have the built up for trust, a story. His documentation on the subject of the earth not being a globe was quite good. But if you watch some other documentations he made, or talks he gave, their just full of information that no sane person could ever believe. For example "Human History & The Bible". People were stoning him with comments, for this video he posted on you tube, it was devastating and still he did not yield. He takes a lot of aim at Jesus. Which tells us that his spirit is on the wrong side of the two lines. The very way he talks of Jesus shows his Jezebel connection. Get this into your head, who ever is against Jesus, is on the wrong side. If its not motivated by some corrupt institution, then they are spiritually on the dark side. Even if someone can not believe that Jesus is God, and Jesus is God not just the son of God; why would you attack him for his extraordinary noble teachings? Does it make any sense to you? Except showing the wickedness of a person against good deeds and words. But he Dave he is, let me quote: "a Hebrew Israelite on a Flat, Motionless Earth". There are a lot of crazy guys running around here in Germany, who are as well quite nationalist, who really believe and think that Jesus was of

Germanic origin, yes you heard it right. It is really fascinating for me. I would really like to hear what a Jew thinks of this, that some Nazis in Germany think that all the people in the bible from Moses to King David, to Jesus were Germans. And if I told them they would have looked the way I do, they would look at me as if the author was from another planet. Thanks to the notions that Western people have of the "Orient" (Remember Edward Said). For westerners the Orient is a mischpoke, they cannot see a difference between Semites and Hamites. They even mix up the term Semite by using it for Arabs, which is actually a blasphemy. Because in the bible Ham was damned by Noah, and the sons of Japhet and Sem were blessed. From Ham come the Arabs and the Arabs spread Islam. From Sem came the Arameans, and God commanded Abraham to get a wife from Paddan Aram in Mesopotamia, so that the Savior Jesus would not have come from the damned line of Ham, but instead be of the blood of Sem. This is very important and significant. This is not the authors opinion but documented by the Holy Bible.

Names must be named, because people need to have a clear picture. What about Joe Rogan do you think this guy is good? How often did he make the devil sign? Its not about us being angels, but these guys are really corrupt. Does he really give you a clue? There are so many, that are becoming famous and are misleading people, you could write a whole book. What about Schnoebelen? Can we trust him when he talks about the highest echelons of masonry? He puts out so much information that can not be confirmed. Most of it seems to be true, but some of it is very creative fictional work. The gatekeepers are plenty. Remember Adam Kokesh trying to get people with guns to the streets and later he got arrested? Was he just highly motivated or did he have other motives?

Let us pick one for the real Patriots. Pete Santilli. Man this guy was on a show. He was like a chameleon. First he was looking like some office clerk with his glasses. And when it came to the Bundy tragedy, or was it all merely psychological warfare? All the sudden he had a cowboy hat on, a real beard grown and he looked tougher than Tom Selleck in his best days. He was riding in his car like a real cowboy of the old days, for his fake drama acting he should have been rewarded with an Oscar. Crying into his mobile phone "No please don´t do it". Judas Jones in his best role could not do what he accomplished. Now he looks like a big manager of some company. Welcome to the "Pete Santilli Show", you have to become senile to believe that this is reality.

What to do with the leftist? For them we have great guys with the names Peter Joseph and Michael Moore. Peter Joseph the father of the "Zeitgeist" movement. Preaching socialism but he himself was living in a penthouse in Manhattan. The costs for such a penthouse we can imagine. And where did he come from all the sudden? He made documentations informing people about fiat money and false flags. But then had to shout out one lie after the other towards the Savior. He was just repeating over and over again. Bombarding the watcher. I met people that gave up their Christian faith in favor of this swine priest Peter Joseph.

Michael Moore was aiming at the gun owners of America. It was their fault that some psychos went amok, but of course they could not kill some bad politician, they had to kill innocent kids.

Psychopaths never go after psychopaths, naturally they kill the better. At the same time he has bodyguards protecting him, and you guess what, they are armed. But the average American is not allowed to bear a weapon. It should be a natural right for everyone. Why does the state or the police have a privilege to power and we do not?

Hyperfascist

Lets come to the worst of shock-troops, it is the so called "Antifascist". Another Orwellian twisted term applied to such influences. They are much worse than the skinheads and neo-Nazi. The "skinheads" are deceived pawns, but they are at their homeland. And for different reasons, lack of intelligence, low self esteem, or a feeling that their politicians have betrayed them, they join such radical groups. So again the system puts out new leaders to supply this group, who are getting them into agitated formation, but at least they have a case to defend, even though their acting and motives are corrupted, whether we like it or not. And such groups will always be. But what does the Antifa defend? They are supposedly against racism and fascism. That is their banner and platform. But who ever joins the Antifa is part of a Super-Fascist group. And even if it might be diverse groups walking under one banner, they are getting financial support from powerful sources. And they do disrupt and destroy wherever they are ordered to do so. We see it right now in the US. In Germany they do not leave a stone or house that is not a victim to their "graffiti art", but really defacing every city, probably in every country in which they rampage. If you are part of the Antifa and you think you are antifascist, you are in fact part of a fascist group, you are just like the one wood stick in the fascia, crowned with a blade on top and stringed together by tight strings. This is the meaning of fascism your bound together with your friends, into being a force of destruction, you do not respect the rights of other people and you destroy their property and freedoms. Everyone who is against your "Values" is an enemy and everyone who falls into your hands might be your victim. The Antifa is a formation who acts in fascist style. The true meaning of fascism is that a few do not respect the freedom of say one person and bound together to attack that person. Under natural law no one is allowed to do so and there is a law of nature imbedded into creation that does vengeance in every case, and it works precise like a clockwork. The Antifa is a very effective and destructive tool in the hand of websters. My stance as Patriot is this, you can be whatever you want to be but do not get into my way, I do not care if you are a mislead baldhead or a mislead redhead, this lines have been drawn forever.

Hand in Hand with the Antifascist groups and radical left goes the bigoted group of the ecological Nazi. The author has unfortunately seen them live, at their protests. In a wave of human flesh against himself. He had to force himself through a thousand of them to get into his car. And get to work, while these brainwashed mostly young people, were demonstrating for something that does not exist, and blocking week for week the city, supported gracefully by the police. But let there be an important protest and the same police will beat people to bleed.

The "Thunfisk" movement is perhaps the first time in history, that a group is protesting for a complete illusion. It is just an ideology and like most ideologies it is agitated by fanatics. No light of truth can fall on these instruments for destruction anymore. After talking to some of them, there is very little hope. Every one who does still use a brain, does know that there is no man made "global-warming", or whatever they might call it now, while temperatures are falling. Plenty of scientists have spoken against it, what they stand against is the mass media and a few paid scientist.

The plutocrats and oligarchs have 3 very destructive groups at their hands and their all fascist bound together, like the old fascia in Rome; it is the neo-fascist, the Antifa-fascist and the eco-fascist.

We have covered now the spectrum of false leaders and shock-troops, from the left to the right. From the very far left of the Antifa, to the absolute right of the Anarchists. The real Anarchists are no "Actionary" - they are "Reactionary". Those that call themselves Anarchists and are terrorizing and plundering are a part of the fascist problem and Actionists.

Talk radio was filtered heavily around 2015, a lot of hosts were removed from the networks. The system ran scared, they knew they had to do something. So the destruction of the talk radio for the most, which was from the very beginning setup by the CIA, as counter-intelligence tool. They knew that a percentage of the people would not go along with the agenda of socialism towards communism. Therefore they prepared talk radio as platform and filled it with their agents. When the time came to pull, they threw all out that did not belong to them. Because the Patriots were on the run. More and more it came to light how heavily the movement had been cracked from the inside, because more and more of the so called "heroes" were uncovered with their masks. People became disillusioned and did not know who to trust anymore, or they would fall for the fake Trump.

Micro Shock Troops

Among the micro shock-troops there are the internet-trolls, who can post, defame, or put out destroying ratings for different media. There are more and more people that do collect information for the system in the internet, as well when they are sent into protests. More people than ever speak against the system now, so they openly recruit people "fact-checkers". When we were at the Bilderberg meetings, there would be always some guys collecting data. They would go around and ask for phone numbers and address. We would march through Stuttgart at the very beginning of the biggest charade of history the so called crown-virus, and once we reached the goal, a big parking lot near the football stadium, we were surrounded at the edge of the mass of 200 people, by some guys standing on the outside with firm eyes and watching the scene. It was like they have been on alert, and waited for instructions. And just before that protest, their was huge protests in the weeks before on Saturdays, what did they do about it? They attacked the property of the organizers of that protests and beaten down and almost killing a few people, when they were leaving the scene to get to their homes. After this action, almost no one would dare and the thousands and thousands of people, were reduced to a few hundreds which the author saw. That foul act shows the true face of the people in power with which we have to deal now. If manipulation of the Yin does not help anymore, they turn to the force of the Yang.

Another thing that we have to keep in mind is the fact that more and more people are compromised and can be used as informants, just in the way criminals are used by the police or FBI. They can just be utilized as collectors of information or be used for a person of interest for the spy-network and their masters above. For the less informed people it is not the intention to make you paranoid or fearful, for the plenty of fronts out there, but people need to become aware of all the possibilities and the ways, these counter-intelligence forces and shock-troops are used.

Ten years ago you could find as much information regarding the whole construct of this world wide conspiracy as you wanted to. But this changed during the years, it has become more difficult to get any good information about different topics. No matter which bigger engine you use, and we have become partly depended on some of that sources. On You Tube there is thrown out so much garbage and fail information, people get more entrenched by false notions and documentations. Plenty of channels with huge following are established with different weird opinions, it does split the mindset of the masses, because the average awaken person has difficulties to separate truth from lies, motivation from agitation. They also are in for money and fame, it does not really further the case. And who is still looking for proof if that new Guru is even telling the truth, or doing a good job. There is a lot of sensationalism and branding used by all the mostly newer You Tube channels. They also copy each other like cats, or should I say rats?

All of this has born a situation in which it has become hard to trust foreigners, this mistrust alone is a huge split inside our modern society. The author himself was accused by some protesters, to be a spy. Not having red one of my books, or knowing anything the author did and how much he had invested into informing and alerting people.
Just judging me for the t-shirt I was wearing with a phoenix on it.

If you have lost faith into your fellow humans, you have to have faith into God and yourself, and start being your own leader. In this way you do not get lost in edges, corners or get stuck by obstacles.

The Trump Trumpet

The Trump was needed to build up a big nationalistic group, that would fight the left which was already consolidated and to split America into two big groups for divide and conquer. Now that he lost the reelection the scheme has become clear, he is now the resented loser of the right-wingers, a good start for a civil war. Another main goal for Donald Trump was to fraction the Patriot Movement. And third, he had to stabilize the United States economy for a few more years, before the cabal was ready for the virus, step two, two decades after 9-11. Donald Trump would become the absolute fake projection for everyone against neo-liberalism, as well as for the so called "liberals".

He ran with the better slogan and thus the race was his. Just remember Obamas rhetoric "Change", but what change did he bring? He has become the most unpopular president ever. Then came the Trumpet with his rhetoric "I am going to make America great and big again". Ron Paul was right, he was in the minority with the other Trump skeptics. Paul knew that he was a puppet, but he wanted the Trump to show it by actions. There is not much justification until now to see that Trump is some kind of savior of America and the Capitalist. The way he portrays himself does not make a Patriot or a Saint. He wanted to go against the "Deep State", just another of these terms sociologist invent, to disable people mentally. A term to cloak highest corruption, by two words, that most people only understand on the surface. And the media repeats it and repeats it over and over again, "Deep State" here and the "Deep State" there, but not knowing how much the deep state – fake state went into their own brain cells. Another such term to compare would be the word "conspiracy-theorist", oh man how we love this word. Even Lionel David de Rothschild a straight descendant of Nathan Rothschild in London used it in front of David Lynch, when Lynch found him cutting his bush. From the very beginning he was a hypocrite. Did anyone watch when Trump and Hillary would debate on television, the accusations that were made against each other? There was zero content, did they even cover some real topics or issues, or any problems they would solve? How can people even watch such garbage without being disgusted and turn their backs on that bunch of characters. Before he left office he prepared everything he could in favor of the big pharma aka poison industry, and the vaccination shots.

Together with Judas Jones the Trump Trumpet did the biggest destruction to the Patriot Movement. One plant goes hand in hand with a wolf in wolf clothes. He deceived millions of gun owners, to put their trust and faith into him, and with his cheap propaganda twisted and weakened their minds. All around Europe the so called truth-movement was protecting Trump. Its all just a foul scheme from the very beginning. They could not bring in another Bush or Clinton, so they draw the Trump and he blew his Trumpet. They did manage to rip the earth for now is a split between the Patriots and the Trumpers. Divide et Impera is the Emperors Sword.

Deep Snowy Paranoia

It does not matter if Snowden is acting on behalf of the cabal or they just let the bird fly out of its cage to do the twittering. The effect is the same, the way the media used this, is devastating. It did have a huge effect and did spread massive paranoia among the people. Such is the force of evil, deceiving and evil. Back in the 90s they started recording and collecting phone calls. Let us not forget "Tron", the super hack who did invent a technical device to circumvent the espionage of the NSA and other apparatus of the elite. This device could have been easily reproduced by anyone and was a threat to the cabal. Boris Floricic was found, hanging down a tree in Berlin 1998, the case was closed by the prosecution office in Berlin in 2001.

Here in Germany the Snowden Case was used by the media and the chancellor Merkel, to portray themselves caring about the threat and informing people about it. But nothing have they done except, conditioning the masses with the repetition of it. They would focus on the chancellor Angela Merkel, being watched by the NSA, that was the topic for months and nothing else did matter.

Before the fear for a real threat comes always the "irrational fear", which then is used to justify a police state, and that is turned into a real threat and true fear. The biggest trick of this is that people once they have become paranoid, will start policing themselves. They do not have to control you, you control yourself.

What about Putin is he really the hero for the right? A hero for national sovereignty or just another globalist. He seems to be proud of the Russian tradition in general. A system of little freedom and individualism. The tradition carried on from the czars to the communist dictators and the system now. Russian propaganda just takes the other side of the fence, only the standard is higher, it is the propaganda standard used back in the 90s, meaning the Russians are not as stupid as the general westerner. However the Russian Elite wants to be part in the future planned long ago, but one in which Russia can stand on independent feet. And that was the case back when they were fighting Napoleon, when Napoleon did not want to fight them, but then went into a rigid hunt, because he wanted to finish it.

And Assange, why did he grow a beard before they pulled him out, in a tragic fashion? Was it real or just a show? Whenever you see a person getting too much attention by the corrupted press, he should be part of the rampant psychological warfare.

Labyrinthine Dogmatrix

Every person I have confronted was caught in the Labyrinthine Dogmatrix, a term the author worked out in earlier writings. It is a matrix of dogma and entraps the mind in a labyrinth. For everyone sticks to one religion, ideology, institution, powerful writing or his or her guru. That is the imprisonment of the own mind. For the most it is not possible to rise above that clouded storm and to look down from that mountain. There is thousands of gurus and wrong teachers out there to mislead and catch the mind of those that are willing to subject their minds to be bound. Because there can be only one God, there can also be just one way out of this. Myths of the world? Do not fall for the myths of the world. But all of this of course needs a high understanding. The stars, the ghosts of the past and the sins that have been past on from generation to generation, make it almost impossible to rise the peoples to a high consciousness, to separate the true from the wrong. But everyone can understand the words of Jesus. The ignorance of every person always stands out and is skeptical towards a new notion, that does not comfort. And if they are told something that is part of the great conspiracy burned out by the grand dragon, they will refuse to learn it, because their innocence might be taken from them, by knowing the truth. Its like touching oil it does not wash away so easy. And the artificial human does only see one face of the different archetypes that make up every human. First they may think you are great and then they see the other face and will turn the other way to face you with their back. He will become arbitrary, because he does not understand his own nature and the nature of his fellow. He might just turn like a maple leaf in the wind, one day your a hero and the next a clown. It is as if the artificial human has no capability to remember, and his reactions are like the animal just an instinct, he has lost human thinking. The shadows of the past lay upon our shoulders and it is not upon mankind to be able to dissolve them without help. That all is part of the great plan, and therefore right now we seem not to be able to rise against the foulest scheme ever, because the pandemic is a worldwide problem it opens the gates for a worldwide solution, the final solution for the cabal. As long as you are not able to see the construct of this matrix in is complexity and totality, it is very difficult to know the meaning of all creation.

The Question of to be or not to be: I am; But your not. Because the question of to be or not to be – is to be conscious and if you are not conscious then you are part of the living dead. Thus we have lifted the great miracle of that shaken spear.

And judgment is a failure and every judging can be a failing. For we were told do not judge others, and so people are running around picking out the sliver in the counterparts face, while their sight is hindered not just by a baulk, but by a huge wall of ignorance built around themselves. Remember Stanley Kubrick, whatever we might think of him being part of the masonic tradition, but he said roughly this, he was working for years on a movie, and he knew it was good, and then some jerk would come around the next corner and find that little sliver. Do you see the great picture? They are not able to see across the two big plates bound around their necks, not being able to see in front or behind. In the end they are not able to see the great, for they can only see the mediocracy and nothing else.

The Jones O ' Brien Complex

The time has come to use the best example of a Conintellpro Agent implemented into a movement. This one seems to be very precarious, because no one wants to touch it. Everyone with sight knows by now that he is a traitor. This Judas must be destroyed for what he is. A Bullshit Artist just the way he was called out by Bill Cooper for his lies back then. And he continued to do so. He could have been the best leader possible for the patriot movement. But this was never the intention. Not with his background and where he came from. Many know that he was lying when he accused Cooper being drunken on his show and cursing, when Cooper was talking quite nice. The now infamous man by the name Alexander Emerick Jones. It is like in one of those Eastern Movies, where the master trained his apprentice, the fighter finds out that his master is part of the evil structure, disillusioned he has to use now what he learned, with his own skills to beat that twisted spy. There is no way to hammer nails harder into a wall of deception. For there are still many deceived by this cheap trick, sent out by the established. And he made a big blast into the Patriot Movement. Therefore it is necessary to build this case up by every important aspect. And Jones is the best example to construct the specific patterns and techniques used by counter-intelligence-professionals.

Profile

He was born in Texas in the closest area of Dallas. His fathers profession was that of a dentist. When he was still a teenager his family moved to Austin in Texas. He himself reported frequently that he grew up in a rich neighborhood, and he knew a lot of his rich neighbors, being into the occult and such practices. So he was already acquainted at least passively by things most people for sure never hear or see when they are young. But this fact builds well up, when one looks closer at his actions and the way he does act in public, on different stages and occasions.

Quite early he got involved in politics and his own radio show. Exposing the most vicious attacks by the Central Government of the United States, such as the horrible Waco incident or the Oklahoma Bombing. He would go to protests and ended up getting jailed, when he in a heroic act was informing officials of the authoritarian passports issued by the government. Showing that America was not a country of free people anymore. Therefore the police took him into custody, which was of course filmed and Jones knew how to drama it up. He infiltrated the satanic-gay cult of the Bohemian Grove in California and secretly filmed that very macabre ritual. By all these acts and some good documentary movies he made, he did collect prestige, he became known to be an uprising hero for the Patriots of America and in the world.

His self portrait was that of a strong man. Educated himself by reading and studying, world history as well as the occult. A Christian Libertarian, with strong beliefs in the good old values of a family structure. By words he was well acquainted to the constitution. He would be the bulwark to defend the constitution and the very foundation of what made America the greatest country in modern history.

This all is of course supported by his Paladin like Aura, and everyone who witnessed him live can tell, that this guy has the charisma to glue people to his persona. People that are convinced of Jones surround him, like the bee swarm flies around the honeypot. Crowds of people would make circles and circles around Jones, when he was at the Bilderberg meeting in London. Where ever he was going the crowded circles were moving with him, it was quite a spectacle to watch it unfold in reality.

He is intelligent and a master in building up a revolutionary movement. He proved it over and over, but never really made something to hurt the structure. Just by implementing some of the great plans he had. He did never pursue any of that. Jones is very versed in Philosophy and the Art of War. So far he fulfills every talent needed to lead an uprising from the bottom to behead the top of a structured system.

He is a person of suffering full of empathy for his fellows. He is completely invested in rescuing what is left of the once great nation, with real passion and strong belief in himself.

He did build up a successful radio program and media empire, and did so step by step and officially without any help from outsiders. He established a well trained team of professional and amateur reporters, writers and technicians that work for him and his media outlet. Many of them working for Jones, many years. This was Alex Jones before he fell from his high ground.

His Goal

His well worked out profile and act is just a build up and a show. This guy is capable of leading and misleading millions of people into disaster, he is a great performer. Let us consider his goal. For what he was trained and brought into the race.

He permanently puts his followers into a state of fear and frenzy. He overboils his listeners, the result is a complete freeze, stagnation and he disables those that he supposedly wanted to lead. It is not wise to report to people in such a manner by using different fear tactics. He does it on purpose. People get agitated by chains of fear reports, of things that are to be implemented or might happen. But a lot of what he mentions lays in the uncertain future or already passed away, but does inflame the watcher. The result of all this is, you become unstable, you hurry into actions and mistakes, which could have been prevented if one just stayed in the cool. He rushes you to make mistakes by the factor "there is no time left", "it is now or never", it leads the victim to make mistakes. At least your inner setup is out of tune, and that is the worst ground work for human living in general.

Then he absorbs, he takes over dominion of the individual, in the matrix to fight the matrix. He takes your time, your interest, he does stress the minds of people. It is the Alex Jones Deception now the big program is running you the small program, it does work like the micro and macro cosmos. It is already enough destruction to become independent to his news and to be aroused by the way he does present it. So he did built up a dependance for his followers. Because there was no bigger alternative news outlet, before Jones decided to flatten it out, and the news became less and less, and focused merely on Trump, and the enemy the left.

He portrays himself with manners, so outsiders think of him as being a lunatic, that is the projection for outsiders and the way he would sometimes behave, when he was to be seen on big shows in the mainstream. Now that guy becomes a projection for the whole movement of which the normed masses anyway think in low terms. We have here in Germany a guy by the name of Attila Hildmann. His face should be enough to arouse negative emotions to people. He gets so much coverage by the press, whenever there are protests and such, that everyone who is brainwashed by the media, once they think in terms of alternative thinking, they have to summon up the notion of this guy Hildmann a projection of foul sentiments. In this way the elite does use agitators such as Jones and Hildmann as projection-field for the so called conspiracy-theories. The masses out there are only capable of thinking in terms, that are images and imitations put out by the popular press.

And just think about Mr. Jones and the way he changed over time. The way he changes his "outfit". Sometimes brushing what was left of his vanishing hair to the side, just the way Hitler did and then mimicking and shouting like a crazed hot dog. So Jones does discredit the whole movement of which he was supposedly the hero and leading figure.

Very important is the gatekeeping. And Judas Jones is a

master gatekeeper. He does bombard with Science Fiction and the Science of Fiction. Building up the fake notion of beating the "globalist banksters" to be able to explore space and the Science of Fiction, which lies clearly behind it. Things that never have been possible and are just fake illusions of a pseudo satisfactory future. Whenever it gets to the real hot potatoes and the fat meat, he starts lying and diverting. He did never talk in depth about topics, that could have freed the minds of his listeners. He even uses permanently certain terms like "the bankers", "the globalist" to brand the great cabal into something that does appear to be something, people will only associate with bankers in ties and suites or a globalist agenda, which does only scratch the surface. These terms of course are repeated over and over again, also by his followers, who are now mesmerized into the beliefs and structures of Judases Jones Great Gatekeeping Games. He will never talk about real metaphysics, or real christian values, astrology and other very important topics to really rise the individual to consciousness. You the follower of such bully artists are to be kept informed to such an extent, that you are informed with mish-mash truths to some extent, to be able to revolt or rebel against the system, in a way to be again beaten and demolished. Because the Cointellpro will not tell you the whole story, just some, so much that you are kept at the atrium of destruction. He will never open another door to show you what is behind. So that the target, his follower will be ripe for destruction. Judas Jones himself used the term Judas Goat, the goat used by the Israelite to lead the sheep, to being butchered. He did it to tell us that he was not such a Judas Goat, there comes up the vivid picture of the swarm following the Judas Goat at the Bilderberg 2013 in London into my mind.

The Summary:

Jones represents the Paladin like, incorruptible strongman, who is on a quest against the wicked forces of this world. So by building up his prestige and fame created a huge following. People had become dependent on his information and sources. When the time came to throw in the Trump to divert, divide and destroy the Patriots, Jones of course joined the crusade of the Trumpet, he was holding his hand very tight. Sometimes he would attack him, but later return to the script, the script read: "Donald Trump is our presidential hero and chosen one to destroy the Deep State and the Neoliberals". Once I even heard him denounce Trump and saying he would drop him forever, if he continued with his lies. But a few weeks later checking, there would be again the old tune in line with the Trump-Train. So over the time the Jones manifested himself to be a Judas. Nothing more than the cheerleader of Trump his buddy and shout boy. He did shrink to real mediocracy with all he did. What was the mission of this duet? To move the right meaning the righteous into the trap of nationalism and later National Socialism. Just enough that were stupid enough to believe into one lie after the next lie, after the next promise and so on by Donald the Trump. And Jones the whole time being his trusty cheerleader and sponsor. To cut the believers off the true Patriots, hopefully the bigger part, did quite fast, so Ron Paul see his charade. There is people that think of Paul being a traitor, until now he has a good record. That does put him on a high pedestal. He did use his privilege and position to talk about liberty. We can not say the same about Trump, he does not fall into this category. And he will never qualify, not for his sell out and also not for his bad character. So the mission of Jones was from the very beginning just what you red. He was to be a Plant in the move towards freedom, and just when they were waving in Donald Trump (remember the old Simpsons series) to take over, he was ready for support. The main goal was the **fragmentation** of the Patriot Movement, in the mainstream called the "extreme right". So Jones was the magnet of pull and he did pull his power into a fragment, as if a big force smashes into rigid ice – it does split and break. And this all was prepared and planned, decades before it came to its end. The reader may take into consideration, whatever it might take to do such a work. How to pick and prepare, the protagonists and how to train them, for a goal that lies decades in the future. Quite a diabolical scheme. Albert Pike would teach his disciples just like a real guru in his "Morals and Dogma", virtues and vices. But he would never tell them were the vices would really originate and he would not tell them how to use their virtues to fight the vices. He would just build them up to think of themselves as being great protectors of a utopian and freed society far in the future. Of which they would be the builders, acting in secret for the good of humanity. In the same way the knights were deceived in the middle ages to be the pillars of the society, to crush every uprising, and in the same way are deceived the police forces of today, when we see them cracking heads of innocence with their truncheons. It does not matter to them who you are and that you are paying their bills, the same way the farmers would fill the tables of those above them, because they have the moral high ground, to force peoples into submission. This is also the way every well meaning person can be deceived by the ratcatchers and frontiers of shock troops, the Agent in the cloak.

Now that we covered the Profile and the Goals of Jones. It is time to have a look at the techniques and tools he uses with his build up Profile and to fulfill the Goals.

Techniques and Tools

Like every schooled master of deception, also Jones has to make use of the Yin and Yang principle, so he will jump from using the female art of crying and whining to become a grimacing lunatic, crying and shouting threats. But everyone who ever met Jones, can affirm, that in general he is very cool, calm and charming. He knows exactly what he does, and what he does say, no matter what he does and where he goes. He is in full control of himself. Every of his rants and all the lamenting is just an act at the expense of the watcher. Jones does not make any mistakes dropping his mask. His acting skills are extraordinary. Mostly he does apply to those that are younger and weary of the way they are brought up by the Neoliberal environment, in which they grow up. And Jones is the guy to fill that gap. He does a great show, it is entertaining and he plays the role of the typical "Scorpion King" leader. A tough guy with humor, hammering every ridiculous aspect of the plastic people environment that surrounds the wake person. In this way he can win the crowd to follow him. The 1st class leaders of mankind are reported historically those that are born under the constellation which the author calls "Scorpion King". This archetype combination does not fear death in the face of a threat and does have an iron will. Most people do not own this attributes therefore they are drawn to the leader type. Just check out the birth chart of some temporary leaders and that of historical men and you will find out that they resemble a rule; *Napoleon Bonaparte, Vladimir Putin, Clint Eastwood, Charlie Chaplin* and many believe that Jesus was also born under that zodiac cross, which is the Ego of **Scorpio**, Base Ego **Aquarius** and Super Ego **Leo**.

Outstanding is how he always draws the attention to his own person. It is always about him, what he feels, how he suffers, what he all invested into the movement. And the usual lamenting of could be better off and richer if he would have joined another profession, not sacrificing for the good of mankind. He does apparently have no empathy, it is all played out in front of us, but he attracts in this manner the empathy of those that are subjected to his willing act. But you should always care for him and hope that the hit squad will not get him and kill him. Therefore are many of his rants and facial expressions, remember Mark Knopfler when he says "ugly face" or the opposite the loyal preaching face, Judas knows how to play the good cop and the bad cop.

But the worst of all is his voice and if you would ask him what is wrong with your voice he would get quite angered. His voice is making sure your out of tune. As soon as you tune in, you will notice how you get agitated from a smooth state to just the opposite. Everyone who does listen to Jones will be under bad vibrations for that is the way he does use his deep and powerful voice. He was trained to use it in a way to destroy the listener day by day. Once you are into the "Operation" and "Show", you will be permanently surrounded by the absolute negative. Everyday being bombarded by bad news that are shot out with the Tommy Gun. A fierce voice shouting at you that time is short so take an action into your shaking hands. Shaken by the guy who knows how to absorb people with his skills. And now he is in your life. And IT the great bad ugly thing – the conspiracy is also part of your life. It will absorb you and make you unstable in the face of danger, literally running for the hills, when the first next bad news hits. Under irrational fear it is hard to think. It is different if the threat is real, then you might act in full possession of your mind and inborn talents. Everybody who does listen too much to guys like Jones and his friend Rogan, will unwillingly let the other side absorb the own life, and it is not good to be surrounded by bad news 24 hours from day to day, sometimes there is a break needed. Especially if the threat is not in front of your door yet.

His news articles are also using the old school Propaganda methods, that have become infamous by one of its advertisers Edward Bernays, which even if it is effective made me skeptical at the very beginning.

Of course Mr. Jones has the power to interrupt and put on hold every caller, with whom he does not agree, or who does say things that others should not hear. He is in the position to smash everyone who does oppose him, once he is on show. And so he did with many. One good example, there was an old man telling Jones, that Jesus would go to people and collect them and that Jones is in want that the people come to him. Jones said roughly that the old man knows better and should consider his own business, not knowing how it is to wear the heavy crown. He did counter that accusation like a trained lawyer, just as it came in and knew how to shield himself from such a criticism. Every author, researcher or filmmaker that would join the show, would be interrupted by Jones permanently, well everyone who talks to him. It became his mantra to disrupt other people, so when he did it on purpose to divert from important topics or themes that the specialist wanted to talk about, it would not be seen as him being in the role of the Goat-Herder. It was just the typical Jones manner interrupting and cutting off people in the midst of important information. Very often it was of importance so that the listener should have heard it.

Another personal trait is the way he does use his Aquarian skills that draw people to him and later disperse people into all directions. So he is the link between all and does so well, but later is capable of diverting the masses.

His workings

Whenever to join the website "Prisonplanet", there is this nice "Dogface" picture of Alex Jones. That is the just trust me look, I am the true true leader of golden hearts. He still has it now that he cut his hair and grew his beard, to look like a shepherd guerilla leader. Did anyone notice how Jones took away the attention from Ron Paul and gave it to Trump? Remember when it was all about the libertarian movement of Ron Paul and it all the sudden became Trump is going to make America big again. A diversion and corruption that many are failing to see, blinded by the heroes shining light.

After all he had David Mayer de Rothschild on his show. And did he not mess it up somehow? People were saying, "man he had Rothschild on his show but he did not really manage it well, he could have asked more important questions", and they have been right. People did wonder how did he pull that off, to get the heir of that World Empire of banking and business under his micro. At the end there came the bad ass warning of Jones, that we will prevail and jail him ... yea bring it on ... said Rothschild. What a nice script one could suggest, with Jones being such a good plant, probably not even David Rothschild did know.

Furthermore he glorified every star that came into his show no matter how fake they were. It did not matter anymore they were all the sudden all for us and all in for the right fight. The last straw was torn apart for me, when he invited NASA aka Nazi technicians into his show, that would talk about the Science of Fiction and that was in 2015, when already in 2013 it came out that he employed a women, who before joining Jones, worked for a CIA sub contractor and was monitoring phone calls. Hence less and less of the first class authors and reporters would join the show, he did blast himself already back then. But how did he come back somehow? It was his Oscar Star appearance on the Piers Morgan Show that brought him back to track. … *1776 will commence if you take our firearms* … what an action debate. And Piers Morgan was standing there like a red tomato not knowing what to say or do anymore? Really, did he? Come on, come on it was all just a theater stage of the two. Every other guest would have been cut into pieces by the foul tongued and sharp toothed Morgan. All the sudden by the great appearance of the Great Goat became a Shy Sheep.

His documentations have been good in general. Except some lies and gatekeeping at the end of "Endgame". But there was this one fatal mistake who no one seems to notice. In his documentation "Police State IV: The Rise of FEMA", they were filming behind the police, at that protest. How did they get behind the police? The whole protest looks to me like a Psyop.

Then there was this debate with the Ex-Leader of the Knights of the Ku Klux Klan David Duke. In this dogfight Jones got bashed quite well by Duke. It was the old Hegelian Dialectic. Duke wants us to believe that it is all the Jews fault. The Jewish Elite is part of it, the same way every elite is a part of the cabal. Many Jews are and have been involved in the Communist Plans. They seem to be attracted to it. But there have been others exposing it. And yes they are in control of the Federal Reserve System and Hollywood, at least they dominate these two powerful forces. The devil had to infiltrate the chosen people, so he did wherever he could mess up the work of God. But there is other powerful elites. In every nation. In India, Russia, Britain, Germany and in China. We should not get distracted by those that want to narrow our mind. Everyone can read the book of Carroll Quigley "Tragedy and Hope", he writes about the consistency of the German, French and British Elite. The cabal does not owe any allegiance to any people or nation or religion. Their allegiance is the destruction of mankind, and nothing else. Did Rothschilds care about the average Jews, when they were hunted down? They had been rather in contact with Hitler through Ribbentrop and his association with the Roundtable in Britain, all well documented by Professor Quigley in his book and he did look into the archives of that infamous steering wheel for world politics. No, Quigley was not happy about the fact that the John Birchers and Gary Allen would use his book as proof, he marked them to be the "extreme right". However he brought a fantastic history book to the world. An Expose of the corrupt elite who does run the world. The devil has been and is using different elites for different goals to control his kingdom; it is this world unfortunately.

Let us focus again on Jones, he has been banned on Facebook, Twitter and You Tube. Why did they ban him? They made an example of it, another projection. Jones running rampant and besmirch everything. So that everyone who wants to tell the truth gets thrown into the same drawer with him, Mr. Ugly Face and Mr. Radical, a guy who in reality is as cold as ice and willing for sacrifices. Now they made a case of it and they are already saying that every "conspiracy-theorist" should be shut up. That is the first step towards total silence of society.

For years now his reporters are focusing on the threat caused by immigrants. The result is that the average Westerner of Germanic, Celtic or Slavic origin is drawn towards the Neo-Nazis. But most of the articles are pure agitation propaganda. And that is another fact of Jones misleading as many as possible off the track and forming them into a fascia. Many of these articles have been written by his right and left hand Paul Joseph Watson. Another well trained Cointellpro, he could not stand still when we met in Switzerland at Bilderberg, not until he would press his finger to my chest and ask me who are you? He himself being part of a spy network was suspicious about me. Which shows how paranoid these people are, once they meet someone they can not fit into the paradigma. Maybe the Mossad sent someone, to control those that were sent in to manipulate us? Aaron Dykes who left the Jones apparatus was very kind and relaxed to compare him. With Watson we have another ice cold actor, who does shape shift into every kind of role if necessary, even if it is subliminal. For example, when he brushes his hair to look like a moron type (another projection for us remember), to then report about radical muslims, to agitate or tell us stories about the braindead Californian Yuppies, that Mark Dice so lovely does showcase. Jones and his entourage are finally a wild formation of hate preachers. Hatred and destruction will be their fruits.

Psychological warfare

He is on a "Show" and leads an "Operation", it is in your face. Its all a show and he the actor of that show. The CIA had operations too: Operation Gladio, Operation Jade Helm and Operation Kill Kennedy, the Operation of a Sheep Goat. Judas Jones he runs a complete Psyop Operation, some of the events he exposed were used as psychological warfare instruments.

Ebola was used to let people run for the hills. At the same time he was advertising and selling his products. And do we not forget his promotion of the parody copying "My Sharona" (The Knack) in a very macabre way, dressing up in Quarantine Clothes. He put out the news headline, saying that it is confirmed that Ebola would spread in the US. Or Ebola would be the "Perfect Storm".

Jade Helm he covered Jade Helm, and how the army was monitoring the areas, where the biggest uprisings were expected by the Patriots and gun owners. Of course Jones had gotten his hands on this hot cable very early. The Texas Gov. Greg Abott ordered the Texas State Guard to monitor the military training exercise of the Federal Government. Again he did build it up and make people stand on their toes. Now it seems to be clear that it was done to be prepared for the future and have intelligence on the "enemies of the state", but they would not dare to already attack or declare martial law. They did not in 2016 and in 2017, there is a bigger plan at work, first they want a civil war to weaken the population, before they turn on the Patriots.

NSA he had William Binney Ex-NSA official on his show, to tell us with sentimental eyes, that the NSA was spying and listening to every phone-call made. It was all presented in a way to just further spread mass paranoia amongst the Patriots. This did have a worldwide freeze effect, going hand in hand together with the Edward Snowden Exposure. The fact that Binney has been again on his show and did claim that there was an election fraud in 2020, cheating Trump out does not make Binney look good. He seems to be another of these plants. All these reports do just motivate a civil war to get back to Trump. There is no election by the people, the leaders are selected in advance. Either you get this or nothing.

The Bundy stand-off, could have been another complete Psyop, it would not surprise me. If so it would be used to first deceive the Patriots by Jones blasting it up, with the Feds going back. Giving us the perception of victory. Just to boost the moral temporary, to later destroy once they cashed the Bundys. What effect does it have? It is meant to intimidate. First the female approach of deception to let the enemy think he won a victory and show the own weakness, to then later take the male side of the Hegelian Dialectic to jail the Family Members and now put pressure on the Patriots.

Steve Quayle who can conform that it is true that they made those colored lists, blue, yellow, red or whatever? Is it really true or another psychological warfare operation. To let you think you might be on a hunting list for the executive forces. Do not trust people that just run around and churn out stuff that can not be confirmed.

There have been endless Psyops he was running amok with. One could write a whole book about it.

His divorce from his wife Kelly, brought to the public light. Now Jones has fallen from grace. First he was the leader and supporter of the libertarian movement therefore, he needed to be the clean guy, with an intact family and background. Now, that he started supporting the dirty Trump a projection of hatred to all that are extremely brainwashed and naive on the so called left, he needed a new background. So emerged Alex Jones The Fallen One. It does fit perfect into the script. Now that he is the bad boy of the far right, and the target for a lot of aggression and measures that finally will be directed towards us the free minded. He is now the renegade who was banned from all big media platforms. Psychological warfare is meant to disable the target. As you read on his homepage "truth will set you free", but not this multiple masked Bully Artist.

Origins

What do people know of Alex Jones and his true origin, except his own words? Bad rumors coming up claiming that he was a Satanist and Anton Lavey disciple. Whether these stories are true or not, they seem to fit perfect into the whole picture, of what we know about this character. It would explain his performance. A psycho needs attention. The stuff he made when he was quite young, was very bad, but later it did not get much attention anymore. Cooper did expose some of his running for the hill fear talks. At the 2012 Bilderberg Meeting the police were quite rough. But Jones was untouchable, they would not even dare get into his face. But they did rub shoulders with every other guy around. There was this huge respect in the air. Someone told the police this guy do not touch, important. The author did notice that he was stone cold and very arrogant at the hand shake. And this was a trait I did notice on every of this cointellpros. Cold soldiers on a mission. They do not care for other people that is their thing. Jones is a cold soldier of fortune for the wrong fate, a soldier of deception for the dark forces. David Icke was quite the opposite of Jones, and turned out to behave in the way I expected Jones to do. The masses were mesmerized by Jones pulling out one of his power speeches, few noticed the very great speech of David Icke on that day. Whatever people might think of Icke, he was always and also on that day he told us; saying that they would put out a virus and the goal was the vaccination. And he did say it over and over again, because he knew that was the next big thing and it happened. Over and over again Icke

urged people to never get vaccinated, and that point was important.
Many people were suspicious of Jones to get into the Bohemian Grove and to film that grotesque "mock" sacrifice. But him being into Lucifer worship, would of course open that door easily.

Lenin said you have to control the opposition, Leninist Marxist techniques equal Jesuit techniques. So we have a Leninist Marxist Jesuit CIA Plant in form of this so called Archpatriot. Like a hypocrite he did stand in front of the Bilderberg Hotel in his movie "Endgame" and shout into his megaphone. As if they would care for the "hero". The schemes, the skills, the training, his permanent psychological warfare and the fact that he must be backed financially, make it clear that this guy comes right out of the cabals heart of hearts. It is evident that the Illuminati, does have families implanted into society, that run parallel to them and are among us. Well, trained with the sole mission of sabotage and infiltration. These families are into it for generations. Jones himself was proud to tell us, that his ancestors were revolutionary leaders. So we come to his personal training, either he was trained by the father or another institution such as the Jesuits. The son of Jones was also drilled by Jones, a clear mirror of the father. His second name is Emerick, the name derives from the German words, Rich = Strength and Amar = Work. Meaning the strength of labor or an industrial leader. In our case it is a revolutionary leader. His father did not choose that name for no reason, it has a meaning to them.

Another resemblance is that Alex Jones was born under the same sun and moon zodiac signs as Adam Weishaupt. The combination defines the persons nucleus-archetyp, it is the spirit, soul and body of a person. Both have the combination of *Aquarius* sun and *Libra* moon. This combination does attract and charm the masses in magnitude. They do magnetize the masses to their own ego, they are pulling the masses together like freezing ice and they know how to break it, at the right time. No matter what the reader might think of astrology, it is the hand of the cosmic, and as above so below. As the stars at the birth so the birth child. Astrology is the true science and astronomy turns out to be a Science of pure Fiction. Adam Weishaupt was also a revolutionary leader and very successful in collecting and charming men. To be a Freemason today or at the days of Weishaupt in the 18th century is quite different. Because today you are not obliged to join such groups to be successful and have a decent or good life. But in the old days it was different, life was much harder and people could be attracted easier to join a lodge and become a privileged person. So the Freemasons were composed of different men. Many were deceived or thought the revolutionary movement of enlightenment and worldwide resurrection would change the old system of nobility and authority into a more democratic future. The author must admit that he himself had problems, to believe that this was true. But think of all the different persons that were Freemasons, all the artists, composer and so forth, have they all been wicked and evil persons? Do creative persons with such capability fit into that picture? After all the facts reported by Professor John

Robison of Scotland about the Masonic structure in Europe and the Bavarian Illuminati of Weishaupt. Robison himself a higher Freemason, had to admit that Freemasonry was a threat because of it being too secretive. But finally the written letters collected from the Bavarian Illuminati, by the Bavarian Magistrate, did shed light on the way many men were thinking and feeling in those days. Weishaupt had to assure his men, that his new founded sect, was in no affiliation with the Jesuits, and some joined because Freemasonry was not satisfactory for them. Now there were many men deceived by Weishaupt and his Generals, and even with his Generals such as Freiherr Knigge he would play his games. He would use Knigge because of his social connections. So the "Bavarian Illuminati" and the Freemasons were composed of men with different opinions and of different character. Some were psychopaths, some were in it for riches, others have been deceived pawns, some were into gnostic knowledge, but even Christians became involved. This world has always been ruled by chaos and confusion. Mozart joined the Freemasons when he was still very young, it appears that he was really into it. Friedrich Schiller was into the ancient Greek mythology, mirrored in his poems, still Schiller was looking forward towards a future in which humans would live in freedom and peace. This two famous artists are good examples. About the nature of their early deaths one can only debate.

Adam Weishaupt a Jesuit trained young man, was to be the leader of a communist revolution. Which did not come to fruition in Germany, but later through one of the Generals of Weishaupt, the Italian man by the name of Gabriel de

Riqueti, famous for his noble man title; Comte de Mirabeau did instigate the Jakobins and with the power and fortune of the Duke of Orleans, the French Revolution was brought to life. A concept later pursued by Marx and Engels. The proletarian revolution was not successful. Thus it needed the Marxist-Leninist approach, which is that of Alex Jones and Adam Weishaupt, to send in men that put on a masquerade to pretend to be of that very group they are to destroy from within. Weishaupt did infiltrate the Freemasons and even the Jesuits. Be sure that he did infiltrate the Jesuits on behalf of the big guys at the top of the Jesuit Pyramid. It did serve the purpose of those at the very top of the structure.

Remember the chain the author did mention before in this book. Now it comes into play again. The Jesuit – Bavarian Illuminati – Skull & Bones – CIA chain. The Jesuits have been the old organization using ancient techniques from the late middle ages to the days of Adam Weishaupt the founder of the <u>Bavarian Illuminati</u> (**a newer sect**). Later was founded Skull & Bones in the USA by a few top <u>Illuminati families</u> (**the old cabal of inheritance and real power**). The Skull & Bones members did build up the CIA to what it is now. An overall powerful spy agency with an enormous network of companies, that are funded and controlled by the CIA. They buy or built up new companies which they front with frontier heads like Mark Zuckerberg, or the chief of Biontech Ugur Sahin. These all are just fronts for the real power structure of a spy and operations network. The CIA the old enemy of John F. Kennedy, who got killed by it, before he was able to kill it, before its unfolding in the 60s. Alexander Emerick Jones is at the very peek of this chain and he was brought to life by it. Through his Jesuit-CIA type training. How often did you read Jones a CIA/Jesuit? The author himself thought of it to be the invention of the CIA, and maybe it was. Because that is the double plays they are dealing with. Send in a plant from youth into the Patriot Movement; infiltrate it, divert it and distract it. And later some trolls paid by the same organization from which Jones sprang, write things like that: "Jones the Jesuit/CIA" guy. We are dealing with mirrors of deception, so we all better move out of that mirror world of bubbles full of illusions. Our enemy uses **images** and **illusions** behind which they hide, their true **goals.** If we shatter that false **images** we will break our enemy into pieces just like a mirror and we will champion the bubble bursting. (paraphrased: Master of Bruce Lee, Enter the Dragon).

Behind the mask of a choleric and fanatic looking man of burly format lies much more, he is part of a sinister circle. He could even be a trained part time hitman. He could be a complete brainwashed victim of the cabal. But he is like a domino if he falls, everything falls with him.

Alex Jones is just another O ' Brien character for the deceived people, a real mess. He tortures and torments his victims to then built them up again. The same way O ' Brien does with Winston in Orwells "1984", he takes him in his arms to later punish him. Back and forth, back and forth goes that double play. Jones does overwhelm his victims with speeches of hatred. The same is done under the watch eye of Inner Party Member O ' Brien. Jones with his specific brainwashing techniques, of using and repeating always the same narrow terms to gatekeep the victims mind into that final room, that does not lead the mind to freedom.

O ' Brien brainwashing Winston after he breaks his will, after the torture he did reprogram his poor victim. Jones is programing his victims. Think of it, is this not another mirror? We look right into it and what do we see two burly and brusk faces facing each other. That is the face of evil and such is the nature of evil: The Jones – O ' Brien Complex. Let us break it with our hammerfist forever.

The Leadertype Formula for Bullshit Artists

There is a formula for every leader, a pattern that can be trained and learned written down by Gustave Le Bon. These traits are, a **strong will**, or at least pretending to have that strong will even in the face of death. And so every Bully Artist can learn that behavior. It is the way they stand, speak, their gestures when they speak, their mimic and of course important is the way they speak. All of them are strong in rhetoric and raise their voice so people will listen. Pretending to be a strong and determined leader and always drawing the attention of the ears by adjusting the voice. Now, they have to spread lies, deception or terms to narrow the perspective of their victims. The bigger the lie and as much absurd it may be, the better it will spread. They will repeat it over and over again until it does manifest. The lie, creed or a "term" will **spread like a disease**, it becomes common knowledge and people start to believe in it firmly. It will become a believe and opinion, opiate for the masses. People start imitating each other and a cult is established. The **Nimbus** of the leader does also play a big part in this game, It is his authority, the presence and **Prestige**. People start worshiping that persona like an idol. This is a kind of idolatry straight out of the bible. Politicians and dictators use the same techniques to be triumphant.

Here are some rules that should help to detect a Cointellpro:

- They try to access your emotions and it does turn off your rational thinking

- Agitation

- Repetition of catchwords or catchphrases, some created by sociologists

- Down talking as if talking to kids

- Permanent threats

- Hate speech

- Fear preaching so to make you run for the hills

- Accusations against you the listener/follower

- Everyday something does piss the Bully Art off, mostly one person enemy (Trump, Hillary etc.), they start cursing

- Bad Vibration, Bad Voice, the voice does change your inner feelings towards negativity

- They make you feel bad, draw your mood down

- They are well funded

- Get a lot of mainstream media exposure and attention

- Supporting or hyping the wrong person (permanently) (Trump, Putin, Biden)

- Connected to other famous persons in the scene, which have a suspicious background, behavior, or whatever other affiliations, to corruption, the occult underground, they are involved in groups that are not kosher (best examples: Joe Rogan, Michael Tsarion, Peter Joseph).

- How is the hand used, are symbols made to communicate to the inner circle (Jones would always make the "Illuminati ok sign" to send a message or confirmation, the sign people in general draw when something is excellent)

- They never accomplish a thing, always indicating goals in the future that they never reach (Jones would collect money to get funds for being able to be watched via Television/Satellite)

- Their workings do not bear any good fruits.

- They want you to get engaged in criminal activities, instigate a fight against police or other groups

- They send you out to actively recruit people for the "cause!"

- Permanent double play one day the sun shines and "we are to win", the next day Armageddon at the doorsteps, playing constantly with the emotions, artificial morals and demoralization taking turns, the result unstable Persons

We have one guy here in Germany his name is Rüdiger, that should be enough because his real name is not known, when he was younger he was involved in the real right wing nazi scene of Germany. If you want to talk to him you will notice that he is very cold and distancing, very arrogant. He could talk perfectly to people, and after some time always a crowd would be listening to him. Sometimes dozens of persons. He had their attention, but instead of really informing the shortly won crowd about real issues. He would always go off into other directions or cut important topics. He did never get anywhere. The people that do follow him are completely separated from the rest of the freedom searching folks. Just like a little sect. So that guy is a sectarian, just dividing and conquering some of those that are half awake. Most of these types have been acting partly as if they were drones, especially this guy Rüdiger and Jones. And why would a person with bad manners, or coldness join such a movement to risk his life? Or at least become threatened by inconvenience of any sort. Either they are part of the "Agenture" or they have a real bad character and are just in for the money, compromising characters so to say.

Is there a short line we can draw between those that are confirmed Bullshit Artists? Fake heroes such as Judas Jones, Peter Joseph, Michael Moore, Pete Santilli, Stefan Molyneux, covering all fronts. They are in for the kill, in for the fragmentation, most of them enjoy to be worshiped like idols. But is there a short form to describe such an agent? The author will try.

Overconfident, shifting, cold as ice, trained, psychopathic, materialistic...

Always remember their goal is fragmentation and the more fragmentation and division they can accomplish, the more lines are drawn amongst us that live to be free, the less it is possible for us to get through this calamity. The Fragmentation we need to defragment. We have to mirror them and do the opposite of what is expected of us. They want to split us. We must unify under the creed of liberty. The values that were broadcasted by Ron Paul or Aaron Russo.

Conclusion

The Patriot Movement and the general uprising was hindered by a few main factors. Donald Trump and Alex Jones, the spread of Paranoia due to mass surveillance capabilities. Paranoia due to the fact that many in the movement were exposed to be fraudulent traitors. Who could be trusted to not being part of the spy network? Massive spread of lies and deception through the Internet by Shocktroopers. Tightening of the structure of the Internet by the Supertech Companies, by changing the logarithms or deleting vital information from platforms. Endless trolls and groups such as the Antifa disturbing. Countless Gurus that entangle their victims in the Labyrinthine of Dogma like spiders. Cleansing of talk radio by removing different speakers, for example Alan Watt. You Tube full of mediocracy and deceiving Bully Art. And this was all done in a short time. The elite had realized the problem at their hands. Even though they were prepared, they pulled a few levers and it was under their control again. If they would not act within those few years, after 2013, no one could have known the outcome. But speaking for the United States, the Elite was save, because of the size of the country and the fact that it is already split by heavy racial division, which only needs to be utilized like a powder barrel. An uprising would have produced a situation of friction in the country and probably is the only way for the Plutocrats to conquer the United States anyways. A separation of different States from the Union would be a good start to sort out the corruption of the central government in the US. The traitors within the

US will try to start a civil war scenario, to weaken the country and then to rebuild it and unify it with Canada and Mexico into the North American Union.

~

II The Idiocy of the Unjust

~

The Idiocy of the Unjust

At the right time the cabal made the initial blast and it turned out that the rainbows made of milk and honey were a mirage. But the delinquents will be found do not worry. The Science of Pseudo, the science of lies and deception, wronged statistics. To be or not be, be a drone, become a drone or stay sane. That is the big question now. "The Masters of Confusion and Illusion", they hit the whole world with their new theme and scheme. To build up a Fortress of Mortification on this kingdom earth. The rulers will rule out who is worthy to live on it, and who shall perish. With pure madness they flood us with sadness and throw us into the Idiocy of the Unjust. Now Injustice has become Justice and stupid lies have become the wisdom of the moment. But who is to betray his own birthright and God given right to freedom and chosen prosperity by sacrifice to this abomination, at this moment? So is evil, in bad times all evil things must come to light, to be purged again.

How did we get here? Not by chance that is for sure. Decades and centuries of planning and evil thinking and preparation went into this process. But conspiracies they have never existed, they are but theories in the nut heads. But what did we learn from Ex-KGB Agents in the recent past, "Ideological Subversion" is the term. So it takes one generation to destroy the morals and the old dogma. People will then be ready to except everything. Every state of total insanity can be given to them and they will swallow it as if it was sugar. The tragic history is full of it and nothing did the peoples learn from it. What ever half truths they might have learned in school, its all gone they are conditioned to self destruction, like robotic machines that are only capable to put their finger on the "button of self destruction". So we seem to be doomed to repeat the horrors of our ancestors, and the past big wars, just as if we were all insects without any human brain function. The space to move out of this disaster is getting smaller and smaller. Soon there will be nowhere to run anymore. We are happy if they leave us alone at home, but where will it end? We are lowered to accept more and more, they push <u>we stand and deliver</u> (Van Morrison, Eric Clapton).

"They will get you ready for perpetual lockdowns, you can not please tyrants by obeying." Alan Watt

But unfortunately that is the attitude of the masses and the attitude towards this system must change, to change the times we live in. **"People will go along with every insane demand"**, Alan Watt told me in a short message. With all the madness we have seen in the past year. And already so much changed in that very year. Our worthy? President Steinmeier, he told us at the very beginning, that a lot of things will change! But how did he know that? How did he know things must change? If the Crown-Virus was just an unplanned incident? Of course it was not all planned, there is no conspiracies remember. Not by politicians, and not by power hungry people. No, such conspiracies they have never existed. The only conspiracies are coming from the bottom to the top, but never the other way around. That is the most fabulous fable of our time. And every mistrust that the ancestors of Europeans had towards the elite for 700 years has just vanished, like snow powder, dispersed and melted in the air. The Joke of the past royalty and nobility, the cracked staffs on peasant heads. Their souls are just blankets to be filled with horrifying not yet written sins, that wait for them to burn them till eternity.

To push such an agenda worldwide, the *political structure*, the *bureaucracy*, the *judicial system* and the *media* had all to be under a planned "Gleichschaltung". This happened simultaneously all around the world in the past decades. Remember David Rockefeller **"... We are on the verge of global transformation. All we need is the right major crisis and the nations will accept the New World Order."** That was in 1994. We know now that this crisis has come to us, that he meant the Crown-Virus. Not the nations have to accept it the people have to accept the smokes and mirrors. But so far the dummies around us have swallowed it and are willingly standing in line to get tested and shot through their vanes poison, from the Farmakia-Industry. It will change their blood patterns. It is all done by conviction and consent. They could do it by force if they wanted, they could eradicate us, or try to kill us all. But the grand dragon he needs the soul essence. For those that are not capable of using their brains, they are no more than cattle to be used as such. They are the victims of ignorance and pure fear. No truth and no good words will make them turn their backs, so do not waste your efforts on them, their history was written for them. Let us write our own.

At the moment it has become difficult to get information, regarding other countries, because of the lack of true journalism and the perpetual shutting down of vital channels on You Tube and other big platforms. Now a triade of dictators Merkel, Söder and Tschentscher rule with authority.

We have an alliance of Big Tech, the dominating media and politicians. But everyone who does disagree is a so called conspirator towards social fascist paradise now. The fascia is in now, if you do not obey the rules that bear no sense, you must be punished or at least you have to be put under the spells and curses of peoples. Nothing is questioned by these people. Everything is alright to them, some of them look really happy. There are a lot of people that will love the new system and they will defend it with force. So long their own existence of droneborg like consumership is secured, they will not care for others. They live in a world of matter and nothing else does matter to them.

Everything that was predicted to us by rightful people that put out works to inform and alert people has come true, and even worse, more subversive and diabolical. For who can know the ways of the devil except those that are in conference with? In some states there are curfews you can not leave your house in the evening and night till morning. Borders have been closed between the states in the first lockdown. Imagine you live in the city state of Hamburg and cannot leave the city towards the north and south without being stopped by the police.

Now we are in the process of getting as many people as possible vaccinated. For a poison people are willing to sacrifice their intact body and health. People say they will get vaccinated to just be able to go to holidays, so they do not have to Quarantine afterwards. The consequences they do not care for. Germany during the pandemic has become a DDR 2.0 version, a luxury one though.

There will be another surprising and ingenious maneuver. And they will just move towards the cashless society. But just in case the system falls we will not forget Paul Warburg, when he told us: **"We will have a world government whether you like it or not. The only question is whether that government is achieved by conquest or consent"**. And did he not lead the charge when it was about to bring the American People the Federal Reserve System, which was built on foul double plays and does not own any Reserves. Neither is it really federal, the losses will be put on the shoulders of the people, and the gains will be swallowed by the Olympians at the top of the pyramid. And just in case the system falls to hyper inflation, Godfather P. Warburg will throw sand in your eyes. Sleep Sleep tight Americans Godsend Warburg is killing you softly. His successor so to say Bernanke was also very open about the workings of the Federal Reserve Bank. He said, **"This is not an issue of credit rating, the United States can pay any debt it has, because we can always print money to do that, so there is zero probability of default."** You heard it, that does mean, the US government can print endless money and give it to their friends at the top, just as they did last year, and will continue to do in the future. But this quote by Bernanke was most ludicrous: **"The US Government has a technology called a printing press that allows it to produce as many US-Dollars as it wishes, at no cost"**. On another occasion he told that deflation could be handled by using a "helicopter drop" of money, just throwing it out to be spread by the fresh blowing wind. If you ever see Ben Shalom Bernanke enter a helicopter, there will be for sure love in the air.

It comes to change the perception of reality. And sociologists use terms to mesmerize the public. They put out these terms for their fake science. They invent terms to make it more attractive to people. Repeat it over and over again, till people are infected with that wrong notions. Like a disease the lie is spread and it does spread and jump like a frog from head to head. And the people that walk around in the televisions, are of course the smart ones to proclaim all this to us. Just like in the song "Industrial Disease", by Mark Knopfler 40 years ago he had a vision for the idiotic state we have to deal with now. But what does it help? Today its this way and tomorrow it will be another notion or thing thrown out. You can never be sure in the new world established of total bondage, chaos and confusion. God is the pure light and energy of natural order and the contender is full of workings that bear as fruits only chaos and confusion, because there is nothing he can offer except death and destruction.

Now, Then and the Fiction

The present has to be compared with the past and also with the fiction. We will go through all three. Something has to be learned from the mistakes of the past but we are doomed to repeat them. We are on another transition just like in the old world, the new world is changed by a momentum. From one year to the next everything is different. And Absolute Indifference rules the masses. The fiction of authors from the past has become the new reality.

Socialism has been humanities great plague, instead of being social it is anti social. Its another Orwellian term upside and down it goes. It destroys the social structure of everything. Socialism has caused the destruction of society in every age and civilization. It is not social it is a virus, a cancer, it is against the nature of things; against diversity. God does create diversity and the devil unity. In the creation of diversity unity is an abstract and sinister idea.

Just now there is an advertisement on You Tube saying, that "together" is the new Ego. Pushed by brainwashed feminist. For the agenda of this century. Female agitation has become our generations Achilles Heel. Feminist are nothing but little Hitlerinas, if you confront them they get really tight and tough. Jordan Peterson destroyed one of those, her name is Helen …, the rest is history or future. That was quiet a show to watch. And he told her, that he could swap her with any other person of the same ideology and he would have the same conversation. That is when I told people, I could ask a million people, how day and night are changing? And I would get a million (same) wrong answers, because its just the repetition of dogma, or ideology implanted into millions of brains. Wired together they are a force of destruction. Only capable of copying, zero thinking for the own. So unity has been programmed into their brains.

At the present we have Socialism established, now the rackets are deciding, what is allowed and what is not allowed. Whos business is vital and viable to society. And whos business is not necessary and a temporary threat. We shall believe them that this is just temporary, when it is the destruction and halt of all independent businesses. This Socialism has of course already brought neo world wide fascism to life, and the goal is permanent Communism.

The 19th century was motivated by great inventions, and the world changed completely within that century. Imagine the world of Napoleon at the beginning of that century. And how it changed through the decades by trains, telegraph lines and the chemical industry. By the end of that century the world in the West was a different one. That period brought general prosperity and people would look forward towards more liberty. More liberal ideas were around the last decades of that century. But that hopes would be betrayed.

Countries such as Germany would see a period of greatness before the first World War. Just have a look at the Berlin of that period, it was the perfect mirror of it. With one attack and bullets on the Archduke the Habsburger, by the "Black Hand", and younger men that were Handlangers for a bigger plot; the old world was send into a cauldron of death, fire and poison. The old slow world before the first great war, was changed into another. Sacrifices were needed to be given, by the people for a great cause. People, were to believe that by one incident a chain reaction caused the biggest and most horrible war the world had seen. Followed after a long period of general peace and prosperity in Western Europe, that lasted for decades. The world entered from one day to the other a new scene a new tragic stage. The time was hastened by the war. Propaganda did motivate the people to join it. If not, who would have been willing to die for a medal on the cross or casket? Professor Quigley did a good work with his history book "Tragedy and Hope", his chapter about the First World War gives us a good comprehension of things, and can be used as example. Because right now we are living through a similar shift. We are into a war scenario, that did within just one year change our lives.

People back then thought the war would only last a short time. Most people could not imagine the death and sacrifices it would bring to the world. Great resources were needed for the conflict, alone between the West and their enemies lead by the Kaisers Germany. Countries were ruined by it or economically purged. It brought big changes to finance, economic life, relationships, the mindset of people and it changed the feelings towards everything. As Quigley wrote the war did speed up the process, that was on the way. Changes that would have taken 50 years were done within a few years during the war. And the normal people of that days thought that after the war everything would go back to "normal". The general public wanted to live like before the war once the horrors were over, and problems were not fixed just delayed.

In Germany the middle class was suffering and had to pay for it. So they started to hate the system above them and the sentiments went towards the right of the leftwing. The Deathangel of Germany by the name of Hitler was already active around that time as we all know. Plato would write about the scheme to establish a dictatorship out of democracy. And that was the same scheme back then, prepared for Adolf H. When the Bees are forced to give too much honey, they become wild Deboras and need to be satisfied by a big Hornet with great sting.

The death tolls and the victims of the war, the shortages of goods that had to be put on the altar of war, the decline in the quality of goods and ways to find substitutes for that problems, and not to forget the authorities pressure on the backs of the public, helped a lot to destroy the morals of the people.

The propaganda in Western Nations would bury all "Entente" violations during the war, and the military mistakes that were made. But they were eager to put their finger on the mistakes and wounds of the enemies in the East to relieve themselves of war crimes and crimes against humanity. Another big show of distraction was going on. Then there was entered the stage of the "Versailles System" and it was pretended that the world would go back to "Normal" standards. When in reality there was another plan under the sheet waiting to be revealed by time. The world did never go back to the old, there were new outlooks and values established. And the plans of the corrupt did take their way through flesh and bones. The path was made for more death and destruction. Within decades the world saw Socialism and Totalitarianism on a global stage at work. The rights of the people were taken away, as well as their workforce and time. Freedom was obsolete, obedience was the only rule. No more prospect of peace, liberty and the world changed towards a forced progress. After WWII the world was completely changed and a new world system established. The forced revolution that had started in 1776 with Weishaupt underneath the eyes and his plans for a Communist World State, of "Egalite", found its end by establishment of Fabian-Socialism across the world. The old slavery perpetuated by monarchs was altered towards a form of Neo-Feudalism. That was perfected and would set the stage to move the world from the Industrial Age towards the Technotronic Era.

A hundred years later with another constructed and well planned crisis, we are thrown again into the cauldron of change. Within a few days in March 2020 the whole world was altered. It brought another nightmare to us. Great cities were emptied of people. People would not dare to leave their homes, because no one knew if the threat was real, most people were scared either by the disease or by the state. Police would dominate the streets, and we were one step away from military and tanks on the streets. People are thinking that this crisis will go away, everything will go back to "Normal" again, just as the ancestors did a hundred years ago. Can they imagine the death and sacrifices that lure in the air? Countries have already been brought to halt by the Crown Charade, the US sees cities that are brought to chaos, by extremist that are left to destroy businesses and property, which they can not own so they have become bitter of it. It does sublime them and make them feel bad so they have to revenge it with their bitterness and low self esteem. That will help the cause of Egalitarianism in their eyes. Within a few years it will be possible to change the world just as it did between 1913 and 1920. We are into it right now. It has already brought big changes, to the economy, the mindset of people and how they feel. Again a part of the middle class has to pay for all of it. Will they be aroused in some countries by Nazi or Commi Leaders? To feed the bees now wasps with honey brought by Deathangels. We have seen a long period of peace of prosperity it made people very placid.

People eat the lies and propaganda day by day. Nowadays they do not even have to hide their mistakes. They use them well to move towards other procedures and processes.
A failure? to support people with enough poison needles by the Poison Industry, for example, the failure of politicians and bureaucrats, is used to make the vaccination a pretty thing. Because it is a privilege now to get in row and be shot to death. In a hundred years if humanity still exists and has healed, people will look back in the same way and compare that two early centuries with each other, and be wondering about the stupidity, blindness and ignorance of the masses, being used over and over again as the cannon fodder.

In 2018 I red Ayn Rands "Atlas Shrugged". For subconscious reasons the author did stop the reading after the second chapter. And thought what a masterful plan for the corrupt elite of today. Why are they not doing the same in reality, as was portrayed by Rand in her fiction novel? Why not start shutting down everything? There we go, they did reserve that diablo scheme for the next chapter in human history. And can we not imagine that this plan is old as hell. Probably hatched out before the First or after the Second World War. And nothing was left to chance. Even the dates and time were well chosen, aligned with the movement of the stars. That does leave little doubt that the elite is right on track with their agenda, not as many that are informed to some extent, think that they are behind. We are pushed through it by crisis after crisis, from decade to decade, and within the decade, there is at least one other crisis. Like the immigrant crisis in 2015, that followed the Libya war and the Fukushima breakdown in 2011. The attacks on the Twin Towers in 2001 followed by the economic crisis in 2008.

And the more we get the less opportunities do we have. Prices rose after 2001 in Europe, when the Euro currency was brought into circulation. Prices did rise again after the economic crisis in 2008, so they did heavily in 2015, for sure in Germany. It was then for a young working person with a normal job impossible to move out of his old apartment or to move to another apartment, because the prices had doubled within one year. By laws put in place by politicians and the machinations that lie behind it. Now its not even possible to have a complete wage, you have to see how you get from one month to the next. In a few years we will see total dependance on the state welfare, imprisonment or death.

Now at the beginning of Ayn Rands book "Atlas Shrugged", a clique of corrupt Gangsters out of a Gangsters Paradise, are meeting in secret and are talking in conspiracies, that do not exist, not at the top remember? Its just theories forever. An ensemble of corrupt tycoons, bureaurats and such that want to rise to power and wealth are talking in shadows about the future of the US. While the rest of the world has fallen prey to the proceedings of Socialism. The United States is the last country left with freedom and some prosperity. But the painting of the construction does crackle for some time and people fear for the bad future. The Sociologists have taken over all positions of academia, press and culture and feeding the masses with the ideology of nonsense and equality. That the human mind does not exist. Ideological Subversion is used to demoralize the public into a state of "Preignorance". The masses have been prepared and neutralized for the big blow to come.

Hence the established Regime pushes through a few laws and restrictions to destroy businesses and social life breaks down. In her book drastically, to an extent to show, the ineffectiveness of Socialism. Of course the elite is not struck by destruction, they live and prosper. But every producer and vital innovator, as well as small businesses are purged. A few chosen ones, chosen by the unknown ones at the top, are to be fed like worms, by the remaining producers to drain them like parasites. They should work for the good of equality and justice, and just keep the failing system somehow going. In our reality, unfortunately they know what they are doing and there is no mockery possible to be drawn at the Plutocrats that smash us, but they mock us. In "Atlas Shrugged", Rand is destroying the ideology of Socialism and its fundamental basis and she did construct a scenario or model to show it to be a total farce. The people lose their rights, a strict dictatorship is established and indifference rules their sentiments. No one cares anymore and nihilism is rising.

The whole system of Socialism is based on unjustified laws, that are taken from the people. And steal the fruits of their works and the freedom to move, act and prosper. Laws can be written, that must be broken, and kill every existence. People will hate them, they can not live by that standards. And now you are guilty by standards ruled out by tyrants. And they have the moral high ground. And just like Dr. (Evil) Floyd Ferris out of "Atlas Shrugged" they might say: "We want them to be broken". They want us to break the laws so to break us and lower us in front of their majesty, and to be glad if they just hit us one time with the club and not the second, cause we have made ourselves unworthy for the system and those benevolent ones that are our protectors. The friends of mankind, sociologists that see us as inferior beast of burden, just as portrayed so well by Rand, in that infame speech by Dr. Floyd Ferris. Because we can not imagine the king to have no cloth allegorically we have to take big suffering.

So we are looking again into mirrors of deception. Mirrors from the past and fiction are drying reflections on the present surface of a Dystopian Unreality. People surround us with unreal faced masked like the Endtime has come and forced upon us. When in reality there is nothing there but faked illusions in minds of men. That make them accept unbearable measures to feed again those that have already too much eaten, they grow big and fat. Their blatant boldness of pompous arrogance stings the hearts of heroes. But would they be so blatantly and bold if they were to be cast in front of us without the support of mass ignorance, that lifts them high up in the air like flying pigs and no one is able to find a small needle, to throw it into their filled bottoms full of gluttony. But our fellow humans they are surrounded by bubbles of fear that make them walk like ghosts of the present, through emptied streets like it was shown to us in pre-programming apocalyptic scripts at the theaters of unreality, which now has become reality.

Vaccination and Food are Weapons

Food shortages lurking, everywhere broken morals and spreading dogma of lies. One year ago no one could have known, into which direction this all would go. It did look very sinister, the weather and the scent in the air of March 2020, were not very convenient. It did feel like the worlds end, it was as if a Blizzard hit us to just leave us in darkness and mist. But Venus the bright star, was shining very bright in those days, like a warning to the Olympians to not go to far, with their plans, and take the people of God unprepared. And the measures that are put in place, are always those that were suggested or told to the public via the media-outlets, that are taking their news from a few big sources (DPA/Reuters etc., Reuters was bought by Rothschilds 200 years ago, acknowledged by their own writer Niall Ferguson). The steps taken are always suggested before hand, with stupidity, the media talks down to us as if we are children. Should we do this or that? And of course always that which is in advantage of the elites plans and to the disadvantage of the rest of us, is praised as right solution, by heinous propagandists. If there is justice in the near future, the author hopes that everyone of those no matter how brainwashed or mentally ill that person might be, will be put in prison, for a long time, that lying destroyed many people, and there is no excuse or pardon for it, traitors should be punished.

Psychopaths will be using food as a weapon. Kissinger told us that already, and it was done over and over again in history, it goes far back to the Pharaohs of Egypt and the dreams of Joseph, very old is this technique. Everything that is vital to humans is turned into a weapon against them to make them subservient.

The school system is an Indoctrination machine you put in your kid lock the door and in the worst case out comes a social zombie. Kids are to wear masks in the school and wherever they go. It does destroy their dignity. Some are saying that it will be difficult for them to claim it back, it could be lost forever if we allow this to go on further undisturbed.

What does our chancellor Merkel say in her absolute greatness, "vaccinate, vaccinate, vaccinate". Kill yourself, give yourself unto us. Submit to our fancy pancy of benevolence and well meaning.

We have seen brutal police sent to Saxony, from North Rhine-Wesfalia, known to their superiors to be brutal or brutalized and absolute obedient. To calm down the people that lived decades under Communism. When they get home into their barracks, they get a bone thrown in front their feet and a medal on their chest. That is their reward, and nothing more. But to them it is the empowerment of being part of a power structure. They are potent forces bound together like the fascia. Just in the way the Praetorian Guards were in the old Rome. And how many emperors did they murder, that did not go along with the shadows?

And what did they do to the uprising masses the Scorpions? They are forces of pure evil, the unity of the devil is their guiding spirit, and the diversity of the people of God is a projection of a worthless enemy to them. It was brought to light their in the middle of Saxony.

The first and only big stars that came out and did protest with songs against the unjustified measures of the corrupt state and twisted science are Van Morrison and Eric Clapton. Morrison wrote a couple of great songs that are stating things simply as they are. From their stand point it is quite something, because both have been knighted previously by the so called "Windsors". Now there is already news articles branding them as "conspiracists", but gladly Morrison refused to remove the songs. This was written by Natalie commenting it, on "songtexte.com", the author translates it: **"So far everything seems to be alright. Only as long, as one does not look at the song text. There the two are positioning themselves clearly against science and politics. They criticize the Corona-Measures and show themselves to be Corona-Deniers."** That is the attitude of our time. Politics and Science have established themselves as infallible gods. They are not to be questioned anymore. Even if the real scientists are not in line with them. And even if their politics make no sense, and are against any order or nature. Everyone questioning the new gods, must be termed as a heretic.

The pistol and bullets were constructed by its maker to hit its target the society. Always remember history. It is vital to understand what is going on around us in present, it is a present of our ancestors left for us, to use it wisely. We are into WW III right now, this is it. That is the third world war, just compare it to the first and you will know it. It is a full scale war not leaving a single nation out. The letter written by Albert Pike about the three world wars and their proceedings is becoming a bitter truth. They are using the forces of nihilism in form of brutal obedient police and the Antifa, just as it was mentioned in the letter of Pike to crush Christians. History does teach us when the Communists first came in, there was a huge slaughter, as soon as they were in full control. They killed plenty of those that stood against their system.

The fashion of destruction is made in the most absurd manner. It can be somehow understood that most people did not get the cataclysmic effect of the fall of the world trade centers and the plot that was done by the hands of the cabal. But how are they not able to see that this Bullshit Virus is a complete hoax in all of its absurdity, confusion, nothing does make sense. This takeover does really show the disgust the devil has for humanity. He is mocking us and taking us in the most absurd manner into his claws to devour whatever he can, because he is on short time. Jesus said he will rage around and devour what ever he can, like a roaring lion. That is the devils most disgusting mockery of humanity, the pain is caused on behalf of the Patriots that can see through this very thin illusion. To be taken into custody by such Idiocy, the Idiocy of the Unjust it must be called.

What are the goals of the elite? Temporary goals and future goals. Let us consider a few things here since there has been written and documented already so much about it. The Plutocrats have already through their lackeys done a lot of destruction and it will be impossible to go back to the old way of living. Not without huge sacrifices and a lot of burning. Way too many people are infected to evade it without big losses and demolition.

We see the destruction of society as it was. A disruption of society, by rules of distancing. Communication between people has been cut to a minimum. The deletion of individuality, free enterprise and the markets. We are now into a planned socialistic economic system. Monopolies will become bigger and thrive. State control has increased and will not stop there. All the businesses that go bankrupt will be closed, or taken over by banks or big business. In the best case they will be admitted to get a loan from a bank to continue, now under pressure of repayment. That is the future for business. The big ones will be able to take over very soon, the whole economy can be taken by them. A digital currency will end privacy of ownership and make it transparent for the state. People will be made completely independent and subservient to the state. Either you go along with what your are told, or you do not get your check. The basic income will be given each month, and you will start at zero at the next month. So like a little rodent you will be put into a wheel every month and have to pedal to get through, but you will never have any peace or security. You will be under permanent pressure to get from month to month, unless your not primitive or dull. We will see the end of privacy in any aspect. People will be stripped down of all kinds of freedom. We are already under hardcore tyranny. But there are no limits, to psychopaths the sky is the limit. The vaccination will be altering humans into something different, and the dreams of the scientists of the past, the "Great Britons", the Huxleys, Darwins and Galtons they will come to light. They have written enough for it in preparation, in theory the elite is always at least 200 hundreds years ahead. And so is the true philosopher, the difference is that the philosopher thinks for the good of the people, while the elite thinks only for their own good. The visions for a better world have never been given a chance, they have always been betrayed. The possibilities for prosperity, peace and a very good life, have never been better, but we are not allowed to grab it and so it does vanish in sight of our eyes. A world that could fulfill all the dreams of the past and a heaven on earth. The shades of the pillars of power that have been build by the masons everywhere are like prison rods surrounding us. They are the not solid prison walls another trick of perception.

"The real evolution of Mankind"? Speaking cynical will become the Borgs. To be or not to be? They will become something else. The plastic human being, that has developed from the normed human, will become the complete artificial human. All under the supervision of the sociologists. And all natural humans have to make room for that to fulfill. There will be a superclass of masters at the top and underneath them a well regulated mass of Borgbees, that will be controlled by a structure of Borgdrones or robots.

The big letter G in the Freemasons symbol deep meaning is another. The skull head is in Aramaic the Golgulta or Golgotha, where they nailed the savior to the cross. It is the skull of a human being and a symbol for the death of gods creation, through the servants of the nefilim, meaning the fallen one in Aramaic. Through endless chaos et ordo by the means of playing out the Hegelian Dialectic, the control of two opposing forces that goal must be reached. You may also connect it to the Order of the Skull & Bones and imagine the infamous picture which depicts Bush and his fellows posing with a skull in their midst. And always think of the G of Geronimo the brave Native as a symbol of the strength that lies within our species, and which they allegedly now possess for their own dark rituals. It is that very Bush family that sinister bloodline that was responsible to develop the nuclear bomb, the thermonuclear bomb, and that were involved in the killing of John F. Kennedy, the last one that came to power to really bring their sinister plans to a halt. Prescott Bush part of the very unknown Pilgrim Society, was steering regarding to Quigley the development of this destructive weapon, which achieved for the elite, a power of pressure, a power vacuum of monstrous proportions. By taking us into a grip the Hegelian movement of the Capitalist West versus the Communist East. And that vacuum of fear under pressure of a nuclear devastation and extinction of humanity was a mega tool to their ambitions.

They are the builders of Pyramids, Trapezoids, Obelisk, Cubes, Circles and Globes. The embodiment of their knowledge and power is concealed within those objects.

These are the works of perfect planning of society. Structures that were made by the hands of the masons, all under the unseeing eyes and the blindness of the masses. A Gnosis hidden under the rags. The Pythagorean System of knowledge was the basis to accomplish all the civilizations that did help to dig the great grave. And one after the other was destroyed to bring to live another one out of the ashes of destruction, there was always an upgrade to more power and technology. Each of theses structures was made for different purposes. But they were all made by the hands of men to further the annihilation of mankind. For each contains a system for the system to be conducted, so to maintain power over the people. So do not fall for that objects that are not the inventions of god. Because they have been inspired from underneath the earth. God in contrast to those that are in rebellion against him and his natural order of things, does create things perfect in another sense. The creations of god do not match up with the creations made by man. Perfect Cubes, Squares, Triangles and Globes. These are seen by mankind as the objects of perfection. But that is the perception of artificial thinking. God does create everything perfect by diversity and not by norm. There are no perfect lines, or equal legs as conceived by the builders of societies. There is natural perfection in everything by its own beauty. But where in nature do you see a globe, a cube or a pyramid? These are false notions for perfection a corruption of mind. And they have brought to light the biggest lies and deceptions of mankind. So now imagine that god has created the earth as a globe. Does it make sense to you? And why would he even do it? Of course there had to be the great

Pseudo Invention of Gravity. The apple that fell down on Newtons head, did not fall because of gravity. The apple did fall because of the its own weight. You do not have to be very bright to come to that conclusion. But if the world was a globe then you had to conceive some new Science of Fiction to explain it to the people, and make it look reliable. Science has become through the agents of enlightenment, the new religion of our age. Do not dare to question it, and that is the basis for the tyranny we have to bear now upon our shoulders. It turns out that a great part of Science of our time is just Pseudo Sciences. And its main goal was to distance us from our Creator, all in the minds of the creators of artificial structures, societies, civilizations perfected by them, by using the concepts of the old Pythagoras against mankind. Science and technology, and knowledge has so become a desolater and the earth a desolation. Their teachings have taken mankind from its upper place on this earth and reduced it to something that is worthless and worth to be broken and just vanish in favor of a nature that was made for mankind. But mankind has to be subjected to nature, which was conceived by God to be a subject for mankind to improve live and to be mastered by men. Also it did make the earth smaller than it really is. So they can go to places outside of the known earth and underneath the earth, and hide and scheme.

The artificial human will counter by saying, that the bee does create perfect structured cubicles and the spider does create perfect looking webs. And that the shell does produce perfectly round pearls. To them I say this, the bee is constructing her own workers prison to collect honey for the bee queen and the spider does web to entangle her victims. Just in the way the bees of humanity are building their own prisons with their very own hands and are hunted down by the webs of the big spider that does web the structures that entangle the world in her web. And the pearls of the shell are the fruit of that shell. These are objects to be copied by the elite to become their symbols of power. The bee, the honeycomb and the shell. Where do we see those symbols that surround us to remember our subconscious of our position of servitude and slavery to the great unknown power underneath the shades of society? And the shades of great creations and principles the Pyramids, Trapezoid, Obelisk and Cubes. These are the shadows of power in contrast to the genuine creatures that God has made. Endless forms of live are build into creation. Millions of flora and wildlife, terrains and stones. Millions of diverse shapes and creations and colors. Millions of gems are proof of the diversity and beauty that are imbedded into all creation. The crystals on the gemstones are little cells that mirror endless and trillions of sparkling glitter and the souls that are entrapped in them. They are the true symbols of gods creation of diversity, beauty and color; and it is a belief that god is living in the stones.

~

III Freedom or Death
before the Edge of Time

~

Before the Edge of Time

We are moving closer and closer towards the end of this world. The grip of the fallen one is tightening. Desperation and evil is rising, all levers have been brought into place to heat up this cauldron of different false religions and ideologies into a great cataclysmic paradigma. All the false religions are thirsty to conquer the freedom of the free. Whether its the ones proclaiming to be for the green of the earth or if they are holding up green flags and swords on it. They are on the march and ready to take over. The masons prepared it long ago this cauldron of chaos. Its ready to explode into all directions.

Wars are looming, we are hearing of wars and rumors of wars. Chinese soldiers are moving supposedly to the borders of Belarussia, and Nato soldiers and mercenary support the border of Ukraine and other Nato members. The Russians with their leader Dugin are proclaiming themselves to be the forces of the Archangel Michael. They are fighting the devils forces, who are forcing humanity into submission.

But let us not be fooled by such speech it might be all just rhetoric to win the hearts and the workforce of the Russian peoples. Underneath that Christian face there might be hiding the grimace of lunatic globalism.

Who knows on which side Putin does play after being trained by the German Spy Kingpins of the Secret Police. And after all being picked by the Russian Elite or maybe even by inner circles of the worlds elite to be a modern Russian Tzarist. There needed to be a powerforce to pressure the European states into the Pan-Europe dreamed of by

Kalergi. The Russian bear has been awakened thats for sure. And what if he stops at the very city of Berlin again, "the city of the bear". And we do not know if the heart of the Scorpion King Putin does beat for the Lord of the Hearts or the Lord of the Flys.

At this precarious crossroad it must be now that we sharpen our minds. And ready ourselves to be led by the light, the righteousness and the pure heart of our Savior. We cannot fall for lies of deception, stereotypes that are in want to put our mind under psychologic warfare to be framed and pulled into the wrong directions and notions. Therefore the author of this book is going to lay out a path to be taken by those willing to run for freedom and faith, instead into the abyss of death and destruction. The heart is free as depicted in a very grave manner by Mr. Gibson, just to portray the struggle for survival and freedom, the prize people have been paying for centuries. Your heart is free and you have a freewill to decide, now has come the time to draw the line, so the wicked, dare not to cross it. We are willing to stand tall, we are willing to die for freedom and eternal life. Instead to be cheated into the death and the neverending darkness of the opposing forces of evil.

Evil is blinded permanently, by the forces that are its stronghold. So it will pursue the goals long written into stones, by their ancestors.

They need to get as many people as possible worshiping the fallen, and as many peoples souls as possible as sacrifice to be burnt eternal, because they will be foolish enough to give too much value to this life. They gave themselves willingly away to being shot by a poison that runs now through their vanes. Many of them just to go to the holidays. The holidays were holy to them, more than the own body.

We are relieved from this situation because many brave people, were refusing to take the poison-shot. And said no to slavery. Therefore we enter now the 3rd stage of this construct. Remember the words of Albert Pike, nihilism and the different faiths spread by the Masons will be hauled at the Christians.

The eyes of fear want you to lock yourself up mentally and against every good spirit. You shall be the victim, but be ready to break every wrong mindset and ideology. Stop following heroes that are presented by the trumpeters, wherever you look. The only hero waiting for us is the son of man. Until then you have to become your own leader. Build up your faith for good, take the bible into your hand and pray so the lord may give you the mercy of the true faith. Because whatever you believe will shape your consciousness, your consciousness will determine your perception and shape the world around you. If you believe in idolatry you will fall. Idolatry of the new time are false leaders, false teachings. The politicians of our times, the media, the stars that are pushing the politics of liberal destruction. Hitler was such an Idol. The Nationalsocialist were really just taking him as a present God, and he was used by fallen Angels as fleshly decoy and taken over, an Idol for idolatry a sin, mentioned over and over again in the bible. Modern people think of these topics as things of the past, but they are present more now than ever. Once he had fulfilled his purpose and driven million people into madness, death and destruction was following. He had done the great work of the devils. And was of no use anymore. Therefore becoming sick and powerless, at his height of power he was driven like a madman and full of energy.

The action of killing millions and millions of people, using his apparatus of willful or forced Germans and others submitting to this ideology of death, brought back the reaction. All the death caused first by the Nazis blew back in their face when the Red Army started crossing the rivers. Its the principle of Action and Reaction. Hitler did reap his own harvest of pain and desolation and bring it to the German Nation.

So never fall for people with too much power and force behind them, such as a Trump, Musk or Putin. By deeds they have to show if they are on the right side. Stay suspicious until the mask has been dropped. They need to be judged by their fruits, not by the temporary status and show.

People who are still living in the neverland of oblivion are in need to challenge their own personal worldview.

Often it has been the fear killing humans. And quite often bravery has saved a lot. Bravery is better than fear.

Morals of Mankind

Let us state some Morals of Mankind against the Morals and Dogma of the Masons. Who are nothing else than builders of Prison Walls. The Same **walls** must be broken by the **echoes**, that have been the choir of the band Pink Floyd. They have been a result of the subconscious mind working for thousands of years to break the walls and the chains.

People need to realize that this masonic system is very old. Older than the pyramids of Egypt. It has been an everlasting seal. And the prison guards have the keys to move in or out of this prison.

Therefore our Saviour needed to sacrifice himself on the cross to be the lamb. The lamb mentioned by the old Enoch in the oldest writings.

Remember the words of Jesus, before the world he said I am. This man of light is the great mystery behind everything. And if we follow this mystery and the words he spoke, we will find the truth. There is only this one path of wisdom against millions of paths into oblivion and madness.

We are in need of a few principles:

Put all your faith and heart into the Lord. Do not fear death. Pursue the truth.

All other religions and teachings will lead to death and destruction, you cannot save yourself with atheism, or by believing that the earth itself must be saved, joining a group to believe they are really against fascist, using the same force against all outsider and becoming the hyper-fascist.

No Buddha, Mohammed and Krishna is going to save you. They are all false Idols. God is not forbidding false gods for his own sake, he does it so we are protected and for the sake of humanity. The first law of the 10 of Moses is therefore a shield. No doctor will save you from condemnation if he triggers you with a needle or even worse an implant.

Proof every controversy, without that principle there will never be peace or something even close to democracy. There are plenty of controversial topics around nowadays, and they are all, already fully buried by experts. Because the biggest lies of our times need not to be discussed, because they have been picked and determined already for mankind. Therefore all discussions are forbidden and banned. No matter what bigger platform you enter, or which small room of ignorant people you might walk in.

Does your fellow value you and your freedom? If not either you talk to that fellow or you must shield yourself and maybe even avoid such characters. Its not in our hands to decide their fate and judge these people.

Do not brand yourself with a mark, such as proclaiming to be of a group, political party or belief. Institutions that are dividing us. You only belong to the son of man. Continuing in this cycle will always make you a puppet to be filling one of the 3 possible roles in this fallen world. To be a Bee, or a Drone or a Predator.

But no one should be a Bee to be a victim of a Predator using his brute force by Drones.

The Morals and Dogma of the Masons speak of a separated world first, it must be unified under the spell; e pluribus unum.

Two main principles rule this world, they are:

Chao et Ordo and **Divide et Impera.**

Its a simple quadlectic that worked for thousands of years.

First you divide the population, by telling lies, creating chaos and confusion. Once confusion is rampant the fighting starts and destruction. Out of this destruction and the ashes rises the new order, and the phoenix out of the ashes rules for aeons. Its the **Chaos and Confusion** shaking the hand of **Divison,** bringing in a new **Order** and the scepter of **Impera** into the hands of the Phoenix. The Phoenix lives forever because its an immortal and immoral idea.

Institutions may die and men must die. But an idea as powerful as this one stays alive until the very soil that keeps it alive is destroyed.

The Masons built a world that has been excluded from all mythology and only the Science of Sociologist is existent. And people only see what they are expecting. With the consciousness changes the perception and also reality. But if you entrap the mind into a world in which there is nothing except the pure Science of the Illuminated, everything that does exist outside is not visible to the subject of deception. Thus they become the toys of the Masonic Order of this world. Done by the Masons. So there is no God, no angels, no demons, no existence after Death, astrology is a superstition and the Science of Fiction called Astronomy is absolute. Meaning the stars above are just there to shine and be bright. They have no other function, as well as the so called "planets", the gods of the old. Which were known to Aristoteles and Mark Aurel to be great forces of power, that have a huge influence on human behaviour. The actions of the masses as well as the actions of the individual.

Institutions are a root of corruption, and all big institutions are ruled by the different masonic organizations, like a spiderweb.

People need to break with the old fashion of thinking. To think of partys, left or right, following leaders that are presented in the media. Everything must be questioned, until it is resolved and stands in the light of truth and justice. The more we are moving towards the end of this world, less people seem to keep an oversight. It has become normal and natural to think in terms that are pre-fashioned. The thinking has become very constricted. Thats the path of destruction. The narrow thinking and stupidity are going to hammer the stones of destruction. Another big wall of deception and another prison wall around the ones already existing.

Break your ideology, challenge your worldview, because the most vital aspects are shadowed by lies and deception. Do not mark yourself with terms like: Flatearther, Nationalist, I am this and that, you brand yourself into slavery.

The Illuminati is not a 100 year old club of old men, its the front, the sword and tool for the principalities of evil, we are talking about fallen stars, and this goes as far back as the stars. Look up to heaven, this miracle view of sky, sun, moon and stars bears many mysteries within, therefore all the dreams of the past and the present are in line.

A lot of people really needed to break their conditioning which seems to be impossible, therefore the ones that are only indoctrinated have a better chance of escaping the prison of mind.

The evil forces in mankind are in complete ignorance, they are tools and not in full control of themselves, they are steered by demons.

We can see the basic principles of nature and how God has created everything. The opposites, there is bacteria but also the counter to it acid. So you have medicine implemented into nature. Humans have learned to use it in chemistry

God stands for diversity, the devil for unity. God created diversity – mass diversity, milions of designs that are, perfect as defined by nature, nature was made by our Creator. Satan the adversary however prefers and strifes for unity. The only diversity created by the devil and his forces is chaos and chaotic, in this he can rule over his subjects.

Contrary to this God does not divide the diversity he created, he wants it to flourish, while the adversary takes in his paradox the role to divide and conquer the diversity and to unify it into an everlasting equilibrium. That is the meaning of the Logo of the Freemasons as well as the "Star of David". Which is a masonic icon and not the real star of David.

There is enormous synchronicity in this world. The way the sun moves around this world in circles, the same way the buzzard does. The same way the stars are moving in circles above us.

Everything you share you get back, whether its love or material things, circles of wealth versus circles of poverty. Thats the choice, if the masses share without being forced, all will be elevated together with this circle, it will float above to heaven. But if all people start taking from each other, stealing, being greedy, the circle goes down into the abyss of the underworld. Free market versus socialism. If people live in a free market they will be holding high values and morals. There is more wealth and therefore its possible to share, and value of ownership. In socialism there is only the elbow, greed and envy, people growing up with this mindset become heartless, materialistic, pinched and bitter. They are not willing to share anymore, and so the fighting starts and class warfare, instigated by the masters behind the curtain such as Weishaupt, Marx and Michael Moore. The children will say there is a welfare state to care for my parents why should I do it? even if the state does not give a damn about it. And that is quite often the case.

We need a solid foundation of truth, so all topics that are controversial need to be brought into discussion, they must be solved by research and argumentation.

Nothing should be taken for the truth until the different opinions are checked and validated.

A solid foundation of truth cannot be divided anymore it will shatter all lies, deception and division.

The Reversion of Marxism

Marxism and all its errors must be reversed by the patriots, we need to draw our line, and tell this system that enough is enough. Will you stand at my side until we make ourselves worthy for the eternal kingdom of our King.

A mighty weapon in the face of worldwide fascism is love, love for freedom must overcome fear and hatred. Love cannot be corrupted. And is therefore the most powerful weapon. And this is the promise for the victory of God, pure love, pure light over the forces of evil and hatred.

The attitude towards this system must change, people need to get angry and realize that things are out of tune, to realize that its all a racket, driven by politicians, the media and the so called intellectuals.

The first to devaluate my books I have written in German were the Professors. They were not even capable of reading or understanding the truth, no matter if they did it on purpose or because they are braindead idiots with titles. People like this, nerds and geeks are used to screw the public.

We should not be agitated by ugly faces such as that of a Markus Söder in Germany or the face of Death and Demon of a Biden. We have the example of the psychopath in the movie "The First Deadly Sin". The psycho tells Sinatra, that he is one with all of humanity in the moment he interferes with creation and kills his victim. He feels the power of death at the same time.

Four Pillars

The masonic order is made of four pillars:

Pillar 1) Money

Pillar 2) Mindcontrol (media, education, religion)

Pillar 3) Force (politicians, police, soldiers)

Pillar 4) The Hidden Hand

The most powerful weapon is money, followed by mindcontrol, political force and then comes the fact that all masonic secret societies are hidden from the masses, or in case of the freemasons the meetings are secret.

If all these four aspects would be attacked, the system would fall. The Temple of Doom and Destruction would be shaken and removed, the same way Simson did it with the Philistines. It would be enough to ignore the first 3 and reveal the fourth Pillar of the hidden hand.

Therefore we are forced to use the money from the central banks. Permanently bombarded with mindcontrol and psychological warfare. We are suffering under the metal fist of the state and his drones. And the puppet masters are concealed within this construct. The men behind the curtain, dont ever look behind it, remember.

Jesus was able to destroy this system of mortification and permanent slavery with 1 sentence, when the author of this book needs 4, as depicted above.

The people were crying out that the Caesar was ruling them, and then Jesus said: "give me a coin, Who is on that coin?" The people of course were shouting the Caesar, and Jesus said plainly: "Give then unto Caesar the things which are Caesars and to God those which are Gods." (Luke20:25)

Meaning give back to the Caesar to Rome, the new Babylon which is now the papacy behind it the Jesuits, the Alumbrados; - the fake money, the thoughts of enslavement, the false religions, the false leaders – present politicians and so forth and reveal the mystery of Babylon this scarlet serpent for what it is. The absolute enslavement of mankind.

Give it all back to them, the filth, the psychological warfare, the mindbugs, and follow your Lord and Savior who is going to provide with everything, because nature is rich. And there is enough for all of us, forever and ever. There is no scarcity. There needs not to be hunger in a modern world like today with its technology. Neither did it in the old days when big civilizations and cultures were striving.

The Nefilim

Remember the words of the apostle Paul, we are not fighting against fleshly forces, behind it is the brutal force of spirits and principalities. The spirits are the Fallen Angels and demons. In case of the fallen we are told that they are the Nefilim. From the book of Enoch we learn that before the great flood some of the Angels took wifes and had offspring with them. The first giants of the earth. They brought wickedness to the world. This angered our Lord in his high place in heaven and the judgement was brought forth that these Fallen Angels with their leader of the name Azazel would be imprisoned. They pledged for mercy, but the Lord of hearts told Enoch, the mediator of the nefilim, who was kneeling infront of him and whitnessed the majesty of the purest light, that they would not be forgiven. God spoke his mighty word and they were outcast, because they had been given the eternal life. Angels were not in need of wifes. The Lord made the female so that man could live on through his offspring, and the woman would be his support. Therefore the Jezebel spirit of the propagated emancipation is also an offshot of the sins of the past.

With the flood were killed all the creatures and deviations created by the intercourse between Angels and women. And they became the demons, and it was spoken the sentence that these demons would be punishing humanity until the end of days when the Savior was to come, to make an end.

In first place Adam fell from the presence of the almighty because he did what the snake told him. Because our Creator was walking amidst Adam and Eve in the garden. The same will be the status quo when the King returns. The sacrifice on the cross was needed to buy us free from the second fall. The first fall was that of Satan, he seduced Adam and Eve into the second, and the third was that of Azazel and his followers according to the writings of Enoch. Hence comes Gods plan of salvation, and this plan is at work. The prophets prepared for the coming of the Messiah. And the Messiah by his commandments, his commitment on the cross bought humanity free.

These demonic and fallen forces are the big wheel controlling the most powerful rulers on this planet such as the Rothschild dynasty. They are behind the secret societies, the secret proceedings. The networks in the shadows, the shadows of power in the background, ensuring permanent enslavement. The ongoing creation of powerful **institutions**, diversions, false notions, false phrases. With words the mind is controlled and if you control the words used by the peoples you also control what they think. If you use the word Deep State, you have fallen into the trap, because this one word throws another cloak and mask on top of the ones creating such words, to divert the publics thinking, into circles of self destruction. The Deep State is a vague term. It was created by sociologists and think tanks, to divert.
"A Selfsustaining Slave" – Alan Watt, thats what we are. But we must be smarter than this, we must be a mirror of our Lord a man of Light, the great mystery of creation and all its beauty. We have to elevate ourselves from the state of fallen into a state of ascension. This is only possible if we become smart enough to see through the psyop-wars, that do occupy

us. We get back to the theme of the planets or stars, mighty forces, with this are mentioned also the principalities who were the gods of the old nations of the world, for which they would make idols. They would give their prayers to these forces instead to the Creator. It is said that the Fallen Angels were thrown into the lower stratas of the heavens.

Above all is the throne of God, as depicted in the Book of Revelation by John. Underneath it is water, then comes the heaven we see with our eyes; the stars, then the heavenly bodies of Sun and Moon and the clouds.

So if the Fallen Ones are thrown down into the heavens plural. That does suggest that they rule the stars, the planets became the gods of the ancient people, and their misconduct for all nations were brute, therefore the Lord cut off his people from the rest. The so called planets like Saturn, Jupiter, Neptun, Pluto and Mars do have a huge influence, this was known to the intelligent people in ancient times. They knew that these forces were active and were taking them as their gods and false idols.

Arameans have always been very intelligent, outstanding writers, and astrologists, not willing to succumb to the rulers of Assyria or Egypt. According to the Assyrians they were ferocious. Hence from this was cut off Abraham.

The Arameans have always been thinking of foreigners as brutal and profane. This has culminated into the Jews becoming really some kind of sect opposing the rest of the world. Abraham and his people were cut off the rest of the Arameans to become a new nation that would only believe in the one true God. Note also the command of God, to Abraham to not take a wife of Hamite origin, and to go to

Paddan Aram in Mesopotamia, and take a wife. So that the Savior would be of the blood of the Semites, who were praised by Noah, and not of the blood of the Hamites who were damned, because Ham was not ashamed to look at the drunken and naked father. From this bloodline comes the Sword of Islam that is a tormenting sting to humanity. Imagine if the Middle East would be Christian, it would be a paradise, contrary to what it is now.

The other line the descendants of Nahor, the brother of Abraham or Abram, made of the ancestors todays Arameans who were among the first to believe in the Messiah. Even the King of Edessa Abgar, was reported, he did invite Jesus into his Kingdom. The fact that the "Shroud of Turin" is valid and original print of our Lords image and his sufferings, this shroud was sent to Abgar and he put it in his palace in the most honourful place.

You see the Great Plans of our Lord are working, when he divided the Arameans into two different Nations of Arameans and Hebrews. The Jews were blinded by their leaders and diverted away from the Messiah. The Cohens executed the Savior by using Roman power and justice. So they would be diverted until today and rejecting Christianity. We can see their Rabbines until today opposing Jesus with the most absurd theories. While the Arameans stood firm in the Christian faith, so the Lord could draw from this pool some disciples for the last days.

To summarize, the Arameans the other Nation formed were heathens, and the Hebrews believed in One God. Later this changed when the Jews were rejecting Jesus as their Messiah, at the same time the Aramean heathen became the first Christians. So the roles changed but God could draw from the same descendants of Shem the sun.

The heroic Israelites and Jews of the taura have inspired many, their deeds and glorious fights against the forces of evil and the granted victories they have taken, with the help of the almighty. The brave prophets who confronted the people whenever they would start worshiping the gods of the heathens, thus Satan and his Fallen Angels. Imagine how much courage is needed even nowadays to go against the will of the corrupted masses, with their blind ignorance and faith for chaos and insanity. The same was the case back in those days.

Now more and more Jews are becoming Christians and are fulfilling the prophecy of the end of times, when big calamities will hit Jerusalem. And we see our Christian **Aram**eans who are living in the West becoming more and more secular and open to the destruction of our people from outsiders. The Syrian-Orthodox Church has become a fashion, and a nationalistic object, an artificial construct of distraction. They have become materialistic, superficial and open to be divided and conquered, quite the opposite of what our ancestors were. Who were willing to die for their faith when the big sword of the Young Turks hit and ended in the millions of dead Christians of the Near East including **Armen**ians, Greeks and Assyrians. We must also not forget that the leaders of the Young Turks were trained in Europe by the same secret masonic lodges and groups from which such characters as Hitler later came. Talat Pasha returned to Berlin where he was killed by the **Armen**ian Soghomon Tehlirian in 1921.

Be like Water and Fire Walkers

What are the best recipes to withstand the hatred and the machinations of our enemy? We use the principles of the elements as elementary.

First of all a run towards freedom, if one person is willing to sacrifice and to carry the torch relay, by doing the right things and even being persecuted. A massive number of us can take up the torch and continue the relay towards freedom. And if that number grows by every act and sacrifice we cannot be stopped anymore. It will become an avalanche. A fiery torch that will spread, a powerful force.

The same is true if you consider the telephone landslide used by Justus Jonas. Information can be spread very fast by one person viral. It can be used with the Internet, by electric mail or using a platform. In the old days chain-mails were forbidden, because one message could be spread like this by many people. To control this the system needs intimidation and law. Nowadays they have prepared by using mass surveillance, such as the NSA is applying

We can learn a few principles of defense against corruption, the wisdom of the old Chinese. They were spoken by Bruce Lee and his Master in the beautiful Garden in the first scene of the movie "Enter the Dragon". Which was really fascinating to watch, as Bruce Lee enters the Dragons Lair, a parable to the evil forces, that dominate this world. There he encouters the wicked man in the midst of many mirrors. So he has to remember the words of his master and teacher. Who told him:

"The Enemy always uses <u>images</u> and <u>illusions</u> behind which he hides his true <u>motives</u>; destroy the image and you will *break* your enemy." *Master of Bruce Lee in the movie Enter the Dragon*

This is the procedure of the Illuminati and their workforce in every instance. They put out images and illusions behind which they hide their goals. We must destroy the image and the mirrors of deception. A psychopath hides his true motives behind images and illusions.

A little girl telling us that we are doomed if we do not cut our carbon dioxide. This little girl is an innocent image behind which lies an epic illusion and the big lie of eco-fascism. The Green Rider of Death, the plague, the new Hitler of the New Age. Everyone opposing this insanity will be persecuted, for having polluted the Earth the new goddess. Another Jezebel spirit beclouded the world and its inhabitants. They inhale this poisonous teachings and become blind and drunken of it, so be willing to kill other humans because they might lose the earth they are living on, and their life and the future of their children is endangered. Because they have no faith in the Creator and his salvation. There comes in the motive to persecute the ones that will not be falling for this lie, this Science of Fiction and Pseudo-Science of global warming and now climate change.

In Germany you cannot even talk about this topic, therefore we are entering fascism because a democracy could only survive if such a controversial topic would be discussed but all has been decided already. The Sociologists have released a new term "climate-neutrality".

How can the climate be neutral? Its pure Idiocy. But who cares in 1984?

So we must confront this lie and the mirrors behind it and shatter them into thousands of pieces, just the way Bruce Lee did in the movie "Enter the Dragon", thus killing his enemy the evil maniac. The same way we must confront the adversaries, the revolutionaries, the actionaries and break their stubborn undertaking.

We must act like a hologram, without a leader that can be beheaded. Everyone needs to know what the other knows. Persons of high self confidence, of high consciousness, knowledge and wisdom. If they hit we disperse like water. They will never be able to catch all.

And so by use of fire and water we will continue as long as possible while the adversaries will push further towards a holistic communistic world state.

"Not thinking but yet not dreaming ready for whatever might come; when the opponent expand I contract – when he contracts I expand, and when there is an opportunity – I do not hit (raising his fist) **it hits by itself."** Bruce Lee – Enter the Dragon 1973

If we were to ignore and reveal the four pillars of the masonic power structure. We stop doing what we are told. Imagine people were just not following the orders during the Pandemic, that massive illusion, the motive was to implement socialist behaviorism and to vaccinate everyone. This Illusion could have been destroyed by just not doing whatever we were told. In defiance to this charade. Walk the path of fire by carrying the torch of relay when the time has come, when the iron fist is taken out of the silky glove. Be like water, without leaders, everyone being his own leader. Finally putting our faith in God and not in the false idols.

To take the path of Jesus and to sacrifice without resistance needs much more bravery, than immediate fighting and being killed.

The Creed of our Enemy is suffering and pain, because they love torture. And torture is to them love.

But our very own Creed is FREEDOM or DEATH. We love our freedom and love goes hand in hand with freedom. We will prefer to die before we get corrupted.

Are you willing to die for your very own salvation and that of your kids when the time has come? When they force the mark of the beast. The vaccination of the corona-virus was just the trial. When they want to poison your blood with nano bots. That will devour your body and defile the blood of your ancestors running through your veins. Make a living currency out of you a living dead.

The concepts above should be taken and spread, we must discuss the topics that are forbidden. Inform ourselves and react to the actions taken.

They will always collect ideas and counter them by using think tanks, that will produce solutions. But the intuitive of great people, and genius ideas cannot be stopped. They cannot control the thoughts of good people. And they will always come up with new ideas and solutions towards the problems that are created on purpose.

In Germany they were pushing hard towards forced vaccination. At the very end of the fake Pandemic. In Saxony the people stood up, what did they do? They went straight to the houses of the corrupt politicians, in quite big numbers. Not doing anything, but the intimidation did work. And the least beloved Saxons might have saved us the day. They were showing who really holds the power. We the people if we stand up together against this corrupt elite and its permanent blasphemy.

The Dreams of the past and the other Kingdom

What did I dream of the future, my expectation was a complete different, or have you forgotten? Why would people be satisfied with what they get nowadays. Socialism, fear, wars, rumors of wars, threat of nuclear destruction. Not dreaming of a natural order of liberty, peace, prosperity, general welfare, the way it was when we were kids and playing. Why could the world not be like that, why give it up to the purpose of the heartless law of this world. A law not following the rules by its maker, but a heartless desire for self destruction a counterfeit.

But if listening to the music and voice of Demis Roussos this dreams and expectations for the future they come back as vivid images what a bless and pain at the same time.

We must realize that this world is lost, because the principalities that rule it, have woven a grip, it cannot be cut by humans. The powers that hold us down for thousands of years are not to be overcome by us, they can only be destroyed by the Messiah.

We can all try our best to hold the line and push evil back until we are relieved of it. At the same time we must try to become worthy of the words of God and follow the commandments of the Messiah, concluded in the four Gospels by Mattia, Mark, Luke and Juhanan.

Therefore enter the new Kingdom of Peace promised to all, who believe in Jesus and follow his commitment.

How are we going to be judged in the end of days?

Only the son of man will know. We will be judged by God, and so there will be no mistake. Everyone will get what he did sow. We are not eligible to judge others and least ourselves.

The legions of evil cannot stand the light of the Savior, they will falter like trees in a storm of light. Love will prevail, and peace will come. A human cannot look into the face of our Lord, you would be blind in a second its much brighter than the sun. But being in the presence of such a light is the ultimate well being. There is nothing above it. And nothing in this world can replace this state of being. I know of what I am saying here. And there is proof in every instance in the bible, when God would be confronted. They could not face the Lord, nor would anyone feel worthy of it.

The million paths built by the Masons lead to destruction. All the different religions, ideologies, creeds. Leave behind all the lies of destruction.
Search for the truth, only the truth can make you free. Stop believing in Science of Fiction, start the digging. All truth and all mystery will be revealed by the disciples of the end times. The Lord has prepared it all, we know what we do, you just need to search, understand and follow.
Keep the picture of Jesus in mind and above, in front, and in the heart. Iam the only path to truth and salvation. Follow me now and forever. Jesus walks in front, always turning back and looking; Where are you?
Leave the sins behind and follow me Iam waiting the Lord is permanently indicating.